I Was a Yo-Yo Wife

I Was a Yo-Yo Wife

VIVIAN PROBST

ISBN: 1540771466
ISBN 13: 9781540771469
Library of Congress Control Number: 2016921570
CreateSpace Independent Publishing Platform
North Charleston, South Carolina

For
Thomas Henry Probst,
the man I dreamed of who became real…and stayed.

Thus, the task is not so much to see what no one has yet seen, but to think what nobody yet has thought about that which everybody sees.
Arthur Schopenhauer, Philosopher, Notable Pessimist

Contents

Foreword

By Thomas Probst, thirty-year veteran of marriage to Vivian Probst

First of all, you need to know that I call my wife, Vivian, by the nickname Ruvi. If I'm going to write something about her, I can't call her by a name that doesn't mean anything to me. For years I knew her by her birth name, Ruth. She can change her name if she wants to (which she did), but it doesn't mean I can make the switch as easily. Just like the time I came home with my mustache and beard shaved off for the first time, I looked so different that she begged me to grow it back. We get used to things.

I remember how close I came to never meeting my wife of more than thirty years. In the old-fashioned world of video dating, we had to travel to an office to see each other's videotapes and decide if we should connect. For both of us, that meant traveling to Milwaukee. (I was living in Appleton at the time—it was a long trip.)

At the time we met (which Ruvi reminded me was spring of 1985), I was divorcing my first wife, living with my sister (where's a man to go when he has to leave?), and running a liquor store for the first time in my life. You could say that I was getting my midlife crisis over with early—I was only in my mid-thirties.

I remember knocking on the door of Ruvi's apartment, never thinking that I was about to meet the woman of my dreams. All I can recall is this beautiful young woman hiding behind big glasses and wearing the most outrageous outfit (which she would tell me later was the latest fashion and had cost her a fortune—Ruvi likes to dress well). We went out to a tavern, traded information, and were both hooked, especially after that first kiss. It certainly wasn't her cooking. If the way to a man's heart is through his stomach, my wife took a serious detour. After the first meal Ruvi ever cooked for me, I knew I would be doing the cooking if we stuck together. I still tease her about that meal.

She's into health food; I'm not, but since I do the cooking, we've learned to get along about that as well. We occasionally remind each other that one of us is going to die first, and whoever does will lose the challenge about which health regime is best for one's longevity (I call them 'The Vitamin Wars'). Ruvi could retire on what she spends to stay healthy. I'm five years older, so she knows she'll have to make up for that time difference before she can prove she's right—if I go before she does. We'll see.

It's hard for me to imagine Ruvi's life before I met her. Mine had been very different. I was raised most of my life in the same city, went to the same Catholic schools as other kids I grew up with, and tried not to let my parents in on my shenanigans. I was lucky enough to get into college at UW–Madison, where I mostly studied how to drink beer (is Jingle's Tavern still there?) and avoid attending classes. Somehow I ended up with an engineering degree and made my way to success in a firm in my hometown before going into my own business.

My first marriage gave me three children. I don't like to talk about what happened to end that relationship after seventeen years, except to say that I think I'm a good guy. I had married young and wanted a happy family like the one I had come from. I would do almost anything to make that happen, but you can't make other people love you, and when you marry young, you don't really know what that means. It didn't work, and after seventeen years of trying, I had to give up that dream.

Unlike me, Ruvi's family moved often due to their religious work. She had followed all the rules of the strict society in which she was raised and had even lived in other parts of the world. She married into that world, and I can't imagine what she went through when she had to leave it, but I certainly understood. We had that understanding in common—that there comes a point when you have to act on your own behalf.

My family was supportive of me during my divorce. Ruvi had left her husband and the society she had been raised in, so she was no longer close to her parents. They remained devoted to their beliefs and withdrew from her life. I can't imagine what it cost her to do that.

Even though I barely (or one could say 'beerly' as Ruvi would because she loves to play with words) got my engineering degree, I'm good at what I do. I guess it runs in my blood, back to my grandfather. Even my father was an engineer. We Probst men are practical, logical, rational, and resourceful. We don't get all wrapped up in our feelings. But it wasn't long after we met that I knew I was in love with Ruvi. My family loved her; my kids were OK with her and liked her kids. I was pretty sure that with Ruvi, my dreams of having a happy family were going to be fulfilled.

After we were married—we were pretty poor at that time—Ruvi began leaving me. I didn't get all worked up. We would communicate, usually end up apologizing to each other for whatever had caused her to disappear, and then get on with our lives. We were both busy and felt pretty lucky much of the time. There was so much to live for.

When Ruvi had complaints or concerns, she wasn't shy about expressing them. As I said, I'm a logical, rational engineer, and I'd try to listen and understand, even though they didn't make sense to me. If she tried to tackle an issue with me, I'm a guy, and I'd do what I could to make it go away; I just wanted a happy family. I'd feel like we were so close, and then something would happen to tip us over. In Ruvi's opinion, it was usually about something I was doing wrong. If I disagreed, I had to tell her. I think that bothered her a lot.

I'm no angel. If you asked people around me, you'd probably find out that I wouldn't win a popularity contest, except with many of my clients who like the results of the work I do. I'd say my greatest fault is that I can be unkind and disinterested in things I don't think are important—like when Ruvi would be upset with me over something and she'd want me to change my behavior. I'm an engineer. We have rules to follow, and as long as we do that, things should work well. We're not great change agents. In spite of my fifty years of engineering, water still flows downhill unless you force it to do something else. There are some things that don't change, and an engineer respects that to the core of his or her being.

I know Ruvi isn't a piece of machinery or a wastewater treatment plant—if she were, I might be able to figure her out. She can be illogical, irrational, and completely wacky (in my opinion) because she's so passionate and creative, which I love. She changes course often (she even changes her name from time to time). I think I get her, sometimes better than she gets herself, and I think that part of our problem is that she hasn't been able to see herself the way others do. She's pretty amazing.

But my wife has changed over the past few years. She's happier (and happier with me, which is the best part of all). When she started writing this book, I was surprised. I had no idea that she had been studying our relationship as deeply as she had. I could sort of tell that she was different—she had quit picking on me quite so often. She even started complimenting me and being more kind. I was suspicious at first—I mean, if your wife suddenly started being nicer to you, wouldn't you be as well? But now I get it.

I'm an engineer: I'm not sure I understand "This One Thing That Changed Everything" Ruvi talks about, but I know that it did change her perspective, so it made a difference to me as well. If you read this and find it helps you have a happier relationship, I'm all for it.

Acknowledgments

In my first published work, I learned how painful it is not to remember everyone I had intended to acknowledge. I wisely decided that for this book, I would keep my list short and very broad so as not to repeat such an offense.

I can't do it. Everyone who has been involved deserves to be present and accounted for, so I will do my best, once again, to offer my heartfelt gratitude while begging for mercy from those I might miss. You are in my heart, all of you.

As always, I thank Life[1]—that energy we call by lots of names and that answers to all of them. *I Was a Yo-Yo Wife* would not be possible had Life not drawn me aside for a life-changing chat one day. What coalesced for me in mere moments became the basis of this book. My experiences since that day, now over eight years ago, have emphatically underscored that all I learned in a flash of insight is true for my life, and I am compelled to share it with others. I'm so glad I took the time I did to get acquainted with my inner world—that even though it took me years of counselling and research, I finally got it. I believe that most 'enlightenment' is preceded by patiently exploring the unseen world that lives inside.

The following people have been closest to my work on *I Was a Yo-Yo Wife* and have lovingly assisted me in bringing it to life. The list is in no particular order so that I avoid appearing to give preference or weight of recognition unjustly. Every person's influence was deeply felt, and without any one of these people, I would have missed something vital. We are called to one another for unutterably rich reasons that often appear veiled but in hindsight had to have been richly orchestrated (if you think like I do) or were just plain luck (if you think like my husband, Tom). Thank you all!

From my youth, I longed to be a writer. My parents, Sterling and Wanita Theobald, not only brought me into this world with a genetic disposition to explore the depths of life's experiences but aided me by allowing me to take a correspondence course in writing during my teenage years. May we always remember that who we are is, in part, due to the labor of the parents who conceived us and gave us a chance to play a unique role in this world.

My sisters, Cheryl Cook (deceased) and Mary Hunter. Cheryl, while not in earthly form at this time, comes alive for me each time I see a yellow Volkswagen Beetle; Mary, has a bossy confidence that I lack. We three sisters are not truly parted from one another.

My brother, Paul, has been a strong support in my weakest moments. Writing a nonfiction memoir requires far more honesty than fiction and therefore requires more courage. Brothers are good for protection.

Speaking of courage, my first husband had it when he courted and married a young woman who did not yet know who she was or her purpose in life. He fought to keep his family together and cared for our children with great love when we parted. When we can thank our former spouses for all that was good about sharing life with them, we know we have grown into a bigger place in life. Writing this book has taught me that much.

My two children are priceless treasures to me. That they embrace me after my years of being a yo-yo mother and that they have created wonderful families in spite of my absence leaves me speechless with gratitude. Their spouses and children have expanded my world in a way that I would otherwise not have known, as have the families of my husband's children.

My writing team supports my work physically and spiritually with candid humor, honesty, and wisdom. They read what I write; they know when I need to take a break in order to face whatever demon appears to taunt me and suggest I give up. These angels in female form take care of my consulting business and manage my work world, my financial affairs, and my travel arrangements and make sure I show up at the right times and places. Without

Anne Wondra, Susan Losinske, Rita Hale, Georgeanne Wilson, (and particularly Beth Holbrook who was the single force that kept me on task in spite of anything I could conjure up to stop the process as I wailed about how painful it was to write my memoir), I would surely have lost my footing. I met my public relations consultant, Sharyn Alden, last fall, through a set of circumstances that still blow my mind. What a treasure!

Dr. Boris Matthew, PhD, and Dr. (Kalpana) Rose Kumar have for many years taken care of my physical and emotional well-being.

This book is being self-published through CreateSpace, a company that is diligent in bringing an author's work into all readable formats that are possible in these days of publishing techno-chaos. They turn on lights in dark places for a writer who longs to share a story but doesn't care one whit about all those necessary details to make it happen.

Vivian Probst
November 2016

Introduction

If I tell you I'm crazy in love after over thirty years of a second marriage, will you believe me? If I tell you that the same marriage almost didn't make it—that I spent years coming and going (yo-yoing), trying to change my husband, Tom, and blaming him for the times I felt unloved, do you know what that feels like?

If I suggest that writing the romantic comedy *Death by Roses* anchored me in the laugh-out-loud magic of 'THIS One Thing That Changed Everything' (which I will refer to as THIS in the balance of this memoir), do you wonder how that's possible?

Laughter is not only the best medicine; it's also often the very best teacher and therapist. And finally, if you're thinking the *last thing* we need in the world is another marriage manual, especially one by a woman who is not credentialed except through her own experience, I agree. I haven't transformed thousands of marriages—only my own. I'm writing because Life gave me THIS, and it's too wonderful to keep to myself.

(If it's any help, I do have a bachelor's degree in intercultural ministries from a private religious organization, and I did study culture and linguistics in order to work among tribal people in other countries.)

*D*id you know that the National Center for Disease Control and Prevention keeps track of marriage and divorce statistics? I don't find that encouraging—do you? They also monitor statistics on disease and epidemics, which could suggest that if marriage is a "disease," divorce would be its fatal consequence. Mon dieu! Shouldn't we all be quarantined? Look at the following statistics and see what you think:

Fifty percent of first marriages end in divorce.[2] More recent studies suggest that these percentages could be decreasing. Shouldn't that be good news? Yes. However, even these studies admit that it's more difficult to determine because *so many of us are choosing not to marry.*[3] Here's the surprise. According to the same federal agency, more than *60 percent* of second marriages fail, and the percentage increases from there. More than *70 percent* of third marriages end.[4] Why doesn't the old adage "If at first you don't succeed, try, try again?" work for our most intimate relationships?

What is it that's not working? What are we not getting?

OK. You probably aren't reading this book for its statistical data. If you're like me, you just want to love and be loved. I understand. As I sensed my second marriage failing, I didn't care at all about other marriages—just my own—and to be quite honest, I cared mostly about myself. I had married a man I thought I loved. I was sure I had made the right decision. Why didn't he understand what I needed from him to feel loved? Certainly it wasn't my lack of clarity! Why were we at odds so much of the time? Why wasn't it working for us?

My yo-yoing stopped when I learned THIS: that the only reason to stick it out was because of my personal (quite selfish) fascination with the depth that my love for myself and my husband could reach if I stayed. After thirty years of togetherness, Tom and I are still discovering new vistas in our post-THIS marriage.

After I understood THIS, I began experiencing such wonderful love with my husband that leaving has never been an option again. You might say I buried my yo-yo—may it rest in peace.

*A*re you ready to go beyond generally accepted relationship principles, which often do not work, into what I learned inside my failing marriage? Are you open to the possibility that the current partner you have plays such a critical role that even if you are at odds, *you need what that person is showing you?*

I hope so.

THIS isn't a system; it's not a program with lots of steps—in fact, it has no steps at all, only a door. THIS is as unique as you and I are; it's so simple and precise, it might be hard to believe.

Are you excited? Are you curious? I'm also guessing that some readers are camped out in the "Yeah, right. It might work for *you*, but it won't for *me* because nothing ever works for me" zone. I used to live there as well; I can relate.

THIS works for me. I didn't create the concept—I discovered it while I was accidentally doing everything humanly possible to destroy my marriage.

*W*hat's a *yo-yo wife?* It's a common question, and I'd like to take care of it right away. First let's be clear about what a 'yo-yo' is. According to *Merriam-Webster*'s Internet dictionary, a yo-yo is:

1. A thick, deeply grooved double disk with a string attached to its center that is made to fall and rise to the hand by unwinding and rewinding on the string;
2. **A condition or situation marked by regular fluctuations from one extreme to another;**
3. A stupid or foolish person[5]

I Was a Yo-Yo Wife focuses on definition number two, although my husband doth protest that he was the string in definition number one during my years of indecision. It's quite romantic to think of him in that way—that he was able to stay attached and that whatever orbit I was in, he always caught me, even though I truly believed him to be the reason I left so often.

Neither Tom nor I consider number three valid. Neither of us were being stupid or foolish, although when we are in a disagreement, we can do stupid or foolish things. I recall a vicious argument over pillows at one point, but probably only Tom and I might think of terminating a marriage over something so pathetically small. However, just in case you think it might apply to your relationship, I thought I'd mention it—and, of course, for full-disclosure purposes, as well. Mostly we know that we were very, very fortunate to remain together during those trying years—to get to that "deeply in love and committed" place that we sensed was waiting for us. It just took a while. OK, years.

A **yo-yo wife**[6] is a woman who gives up and leaves a committed relationship for a wide variety of reasons. Then she comes back. It's also a wife who can't decide to stay in her marriage. She often thinks about leaving and may even talk to others about it but stays for a variety of reasons. 'Yo-yoing' can be physical or emotional. I'm quite sure there are many men who deal with the same quandary, but I can only speak from my own experience. A study by AOL with *Redbook* reveals that *I'm not the only yo-yo wife* in the world. In fact, *72 percent* of women consider leaving their marriages.[7] It doesn't make me feel good that I have so much company.

Like oil and vinegar, Tom and I had a hard time getting along together after we were married. And just like oil and vinegar, when things got shaken up, it was either very, very good or very bad. Often, the only way I felt safe was to separate; I left when it hurt too much to stay.

It was Tom who suggested the title of this book be *I <u>Was</u> a Yo-Yo Wife* because he wants to clarify that I'm not that any longer. I love him for being "the string": for staying and loving me through the yo-yo years, even though I blamed him for so much of our difficulty.

*P*arts of *I Was a Yo-Yo Wife* will read like fiction because that's the only way I know how to tell a story, but everything is God's honest truth. In her fabulous book *Creative is a Verb,*[8] Patti Digh saved what could be my only nonfiction work by suggesting that authors should "write like an orphan." I wanted to be honest about my life, but I didn't want to injure others or distract from the beauty of the message I had received and how it had saved my marriage. Once I got Digh's advice, I was truly able to move ahead; it was the permission I needed to tell a 100 percent authentic version of my story just like it happened, as far as I can remember.

I Was a Yo-Yo Wife is more than a memoir. It's my life story set in a collage of the most advanced scientific thinking, with roots in the deepest spiritual truth. It's as difficult to believe as it is easy to apply. I hope you will join me in this fascinating journey. It not only stopped me from leaving my marriage, it continues to enchant me with the treasures that my marriage holds for me almost every day. Now, when things get tough—and they still do—I don't have to leave and start over again. No more yo-yoing! (Happy dance!)

Finally, if I tell you that I took the journey to THIS *without* my husband—that I never had to drag him to counseling sessions with me (and what woman who senses that a relationship is in trouble has not tried to convince her husband to take that route?)—can you imagine that? I did not have to "fix" him or "blame" him or myself at all, and we don't have to fight our way into some vague, lukewarm compromise all the time either. I learned the real reason I had married Tom, and that changed everything.

Do you wonder how that's possible? If you do, that's the purpose of sharing this incredible discovery, and it is the reason I'm writing this book. Hey, I'm coming out of the closet with my most intimate secrets, standing naked in front of whoever reads this book. I hope you appreciate that, but mostly I hope you get THIS and that it helps.

What about you? Are you ready to walk out the door of an unhappy (boring, miserable, "where do I begin to tell you all that's wrong with him or her") relationship? THIS might change that.

Are you miserable but sticking it out with the same partner because of a vow you took years ago? Consider THIS, and read about the only vow that really matters in Chapter 12. See if it puts a spark back into that relationship.

Have you given up, thinking, *this is as good as it gets*? Think again—THIS just might make it better and better and better.

Have you been unable to find love, no matter how diligently you've searched? Is there something wrong with every person you've encountered? Oh la la! You simply must try THIS!

Have you tried and tried again, only to find that it just gets worse? Give THIS a chance!

I am one woman with a simple hope—that what I learned might help someone else. Remember, I am not licensed to practice any form of counseling or therapy; I only know what happened in my own second marriage, and I think it's so gosh-darned wonderful that I will share it with anyone who wants to read or talk about it.

That my engineer husband, Tom, has agreed to be part of this adventure means the world to me. Hopefully, you enjoyed his comments in the foreword above. He has always believed in us. He has withstood everything my trauma and insecurity could throw at him. Together, we have learned to reflect the best in each other; we are both stronger because we have lived and loved through it all.

This is a self-help memoir—it is a compilation of the events that brought me to a new revelation that changed my marriage and brought it back from the brink of disaster to a lifetime of mutual love, respect, and growth. Much of what I learned is already presented in great works by both ancient philosophers and mystics, modern spiritual teachers, scientists, and those who have explored the outer reaches of the nature of our lives on earth. I have been profoundly influenced and am extraordinarily grateful that these truth tellers did not waiver when an entire world condemned them for their discoveries. I would not have arrived here if I had not traveled with many scholars and teachers. Check the bibliography in the back for a list of authors who've had input into my extraordinary adventure.

If you're ready, read on!

"Claras" Notes for the Faint of Heart (or People Who Just Don't Like to Read)

C liffsNotes®. has received plenty of attention over the years in colleges and universities, bookstores, and the like for summarizing documents. I decided that I would create "Clara" notes for my book. *Clara* is for clarity. Being an "equalist" (a woman who believes that men and women are equal in all things and need to be honored as such), I also like that it's a woman's name.

For those of you who can't bear to read the whole book, although I believe that the details are wonderfully helpful to understanding THIS, here's a summary of what THIS is all about. You won't get the depth (or the fun), but some of us need to snorkel before we sign up for diving lessons. I understand.

In chapters 1 to 3, I describe what brought me to THIS and then move more deeply into specific aspects in the remaining chapters.

So what is THIS? I call it the Law of Reflection. It's not a new concept—its scientific origins date back to Euclid in 200 BC or thereabouts. However, it wasn't until the 1600s that the law was understood correctly, reversing the long-held belief that light travels from the eye to the object, when the opposite is actually correct.

Scientist Richard Fitzpatrick, professor of physics at the University of Texas, is noted for teaching and explaining this law in modern times. He says, "The law of reflection states that the incident ray, the reflected ray, and the normal to the surface of the mirror *all lie in the same plane*. Furthermore, the *angle of reflection is equal to the angle of incidence*."[9]

That scientific law packs a powerful punch in our study of THIS. In my nonscientific vernacular, THIS means that everything that shows up in my relationship with my most significant other (who is my reflection) is vibrationally proportionate to how I'm relating to myself in my inner world—*and reflects with equal intensity*. If I like what I see externally, how wonderful. If I don't, I work things out on the inside, which then is reflected in equal intensity in my outside world with almost miraculous precision.

My external world is proportionately influenced by my internal world; whatever reaction I see in other people (in this case, my husband) toward me is equal to what is occurring *emotionally* in my inner world. The reflection is not one of actual circumstances; it's a mirror of emotional intensity. I refer to the inner world as "Planet Me" because I believe that we are all unique and that each of us attracts whatever comes to us based on the strength and magnetism of our inner world orientation. Besides, it's a lot more fun to imagine my own planet; it gives me an entire realm for decorating.

In *I Was a Yo-Yo Wife*, the focus is indeed on the inner world; the scientific and spiritual aspects of THIS help me to see Planet Me through the lens of what is happening around me in the external world.

*J*ust as there are Seven Wonders of the World externally, I believe there are seven internal wonders. (See Chapters 9-18. I know that more than seven chapters but Life gave me ten chapters to explain it all. Thanks for noticing.) In *I Was a Yo-Yo Wife*, we will visit all of them specifically as they relate to our most intimate relationship. THIS is one concept; the Seven Wonders are simply different angles that help us see the whole. For me it's easiest if I further separate these into three categories as listed below.

Section A. The Wonders of My Relationship to Myself (Meology)
Chapters 10-14

1. Everything I see around me is intended for me to be able to see what I believe about myself; I cannot help but create what lives inside me in my external world; the external and internal are inseparable.

2. I am creating my future right now. There is no blame; I am not a victim.

3. My primary life purpose is to deeply love and approve of myself, to know who I am, and to allow that profound sense of self to joyfully guide what I create. (I call it Meology and devote considerable attention to it in chapters 12 to 14).

Section B. The Wonders of My Relationship to My Most Intimate Partner (Chapters 15-17)

4. I am in exactly the relationship I need to be in, for reasons I may have yet to discover. If I don't like what I find in my most intimate relationship, it's up to me to resolve what's causing my discomfort in my inner world.

5. Who I am in a relationship <u>with</u> is less important than *who I am being in that relationship*. I am either being my extraordinary true self or a hideously false imitation that my protective ego prefers.

6. I can leave a relationship as long as I recognize that I take my own issues with me; they will follow me wherever I go until I allow them to share their special wisdom.

Section C. The Wonder of My Relationship to Life (Chapter 18)

7. I am deeply loved and connected to Life, the energy that lives and breathes through me, whether I believe it or not. Life is profoundly interested in me and cares about me to the nth degree.

These will each be discussed in more detail as we travel through the only world that matters—*the one inside.*

Part 1

How I Got to THIS

One

Yo: My First Marriage

1978, Senegal, West Africa

*Under a mosquito net in a mud-bricked house that cooked
us like an oven at night, I asked God to take my life.*

—Vivian Probst

For those who have served as a missionary to tribal people in a foreign country because it is a call from their souls, such a life nurtures them and feeds their spirits from the deep well of knowing they are doing their true work in life. However, for those who have chosen such a life because they are prevented from recognizing their own soul's purpose, any suffering feels insurmountable.

Such was my case. I didn't know I had to *choose* a missionary's life from the deepest calling of my soul and that my suffering in Africa was my heart in the process of breaking free. I thought that since I had grown up inside a family, a belief system, and an organization that trained people for such service, this was the only true and worthy calling. Even though my young soul had its own ideas about what it wanted for my life, I obediently followed the footsteps of my parents and ancestors in my life's work. How could I know that Life was working to show me my own true path by allowing me to feel so lost and out of place as I forced myself to live a life that wasn't mine?

My husband and I had committed to this life in 1973 and invested seven years training for it. It wasn't like this was some madcap, spontaneous frolic. Bible school, boot camp, jungle camp, and language school; courses in culture, linguistics, anthropology, and field medicine; plus, two years of raising funds for a life of missionary service. We had two young children, and I was twenty-seven when we left for the mission field; we expected to be gone five years. How was it that we were back in the United States in six months? It was all my fault.

It wasn't the heat of the mud-brick home that my first husband, Alvin[10] and I and our two very young children (Hannah, age four, and Lincoln, age two) were living in; it wasn't the snake that greeted us in our new quarters on our first day in our new home, or the dysentery our children suffered; it wasn't the maggots, the mice, or the toads that covered our floor in the middle of the night so that the only way to get to the outhouse bathroom was to crunch through them; it wasn't even that Alvin's five years' worth of underwear was completely ruined by the African wash women who, in hanging the laundry to dry in the 130-degree heat, stretched the elastic bands as far apart as they could.. (Don't try this at home.)

It wasn't the exquisitely difficult task of putting a meal on the table, the limited options for food, the unsafe water I had to boil even to do dishes, or that I was inept with a pressure cooker. It wasn't the mosquitoes that opened their airport runways in our bedroom as we dashed under our mosquito nets after dark or the worms that burrowed into my children's stomachs and had to be coaxed out with pieces of bread taped over the microscopic point of entry (in this case my babies' bellies) so that the worms would get hungry, come out, and almost literally ask, "Where's dinner?" so that we could remove them.

It wasn't even the poverty, the lack of nourishing food, having to take showers from buckets of water warmed by the daytime heat, the understanding that "running water" was only true if one ran while carrying it, or the villagers staring into our windows during the day, quite in awe of what we considered meager possessions. All of this was hard, but it was what we had been trained to expect.

What I never anticipated was that the heretofore unattended longings of my soul and spirit would feel at liberty to come out and overwhelm me. It was being four thousand miles away from the society in which I had been raised and trained—the society that had told me my work in the world was to save others from hell, that told me women were to be submissive to men, and that counseled me that what I wanted for my own life in the recesses of my being was wrong and sinful.

What got me was the voices of the African women singing as they walked down dirt roads with baskets of food or clothing on their heads. *Were they happy?* It was hearing the traditional dance festival one night—the drum vibrations under my feet that tantalized me until all I wanted to do was run to the village and join in, even as other missionaries stood with me, remarking about the heathenism of it all.

I was not where I belonged—and I could not reach back home to reassure myself (this was long before fax machines, Internet, e-mail, and all that real-time technology that we enjoy today). I was compelled to listen to the voice of my heart at night as I lay beside my husband, tossing and turning, arguing, and trying to avoid the truth.

So I asked God to take my life—to spare me from having to pay the price of being honest at last. Yes, at that time it felt far easier, not just on me, but on everyone who would suffer as I faced the world as an honest woman for the first time in my life, my big-girl panties around my ankles. It was completely my fault that we were sent home and excommunicated with such immediacy that it took our breath away.

*F*rom the day I went into counseling with a Christian psychiatrist, I knew my first marriage was over.

How can I describe the guilt, shame, and intense sorrow that weakened me in every possible way in the aftermath? Nothing felt like a victory as I pulled our family apart, as I deserted my extended family's heritage and passion for religious service, or as I released custody of our two children to the man who would soon be my ex-husband because I felt so deeply unworthy—and he was suing for custody. I understood his position: *Who was this woman he had married in good faith, who had broken her vow to him and to God? How could he entrust her with his children?* Part of me agreed with Alvin. In spite of my deep belief that I had to come clean, I couldn't fathom that I was doing the right thing. Leaving my marriage was the worst form of sin, and I still believed with my whole heart that I was committing such a transgression that my children would be better off with their father. I didn't drop all those old beliefs just because I decided to act consciously on my own behalf. It was terrifying to live through them on my way to becoming myself.

But Life had not forgotten me. Even in these dark days, I miraculously found my way to the Women's Center in Waukesha, Wisconsin[11], where the work of putting together the real me began.

Two

Yo-Yo: My Second Marriage

2008, Waukesha, Wisconsin

*I was stunned to discover that I reverted back to the status
of "wife" as I had experienced it in my first marriage.
Things that had bothered me about being married
the first time resurfaced with even more intensity.*

- Vivian Probst

Thirty years after I left my first marriage, I was ready to leave my second husband—for good—even though I truly loved Thomas Henry Probst and had married him as a free and independent woman in 1986. Three life-changing events would hold me fast: the death of my older sister from Lou Gehrig's disease (March 26), an awakening encounter with Life as I headed off to pack my bags and leave Tom for the last time only three weeks later (April 17), and the arrival of *Death by Roses,* a new story that swept me into its arms for five years and anchored me deeply into the lessons of THIS (May 17).

How I Met My Second Husband

My favorite question to ask other couples is how they met. I believe every relationship is a fascinating and cosmic (you say, "comic?") intersection between two people, an event orchestrated with divine intent in our time/space reality. We meet who we meet for reasons that we probably won't fully understand in this lifetime. It is all intended for good, even when it feels bad. In my novel, *Death by Roses*, Art and Mae Rose McElroy are prime examples of this concept. If only we had the ability to see our lives from a 'higher' perspective!

Tom and I met through a video-dating service in 1985; we married in 1986. It was love at first sight, sealed with our first kiss under the watchful eye of an owl perched in a tree above us. Magical? You bet! It was pure destiny in all its enchanting momentum. I have never wanted any other man in my life again—ever. Tom was IT for me, even during the years I tended to leave him.

Here's what's interesting and possibly true for others besides me. After we were married, I was stunned to discover that I reverted back to status of "wife" as I had experienced it in my first marriage. Things that had bothered me about being married the first time resurfaced *with even more intensity* the second time around. How could that be?

The two men, Alvin and Tom, could not have been more different. I would eventually come to realize (years later) that the cause of my suffering was rooted elsewhere. In the meantime, I fell right back into my old patterns of blame and the need to help Tom see where he had to change.

Tom is a marvelous man of strong opinion, and I adore him. He's fun, intelligent, good-looking, charming, fiercely independent, truthful, and completely able to focus on what he sees as his next goal. What I discovered right after we said, "I do," was that I could be fun, intelligent, charming, attractive, fiercely independent, and completely able to focus on my next goal *until I was in a relationship with a man.* Then I lost my focus.

Something about being married again brought up old patterns. I didn't know how to shake them. More than once, I felt caught between making myself happy by following my preferences and pleasing Tom. That's when my yo-yoing began—those were the times I left. There were several of these events in the first year. While the number of them diminished over time, they continued to occur until at one point we separated for three months under a therapist's care.

Tom is not a demanding, self-centered partner—he's as interested in my success as he is in his own. But he is extremely rational, which put me at a disadvantage as a fragile newcomer to the "real world." I didn't know the culture of being successful, and I certainly didn't know how to relate to a passionately powerful man, especially when he expected me to be passionately powerful as well—which I thought I was until…well…until I said, "I do," for the second time.

In essence, the woman I had grown into during the years after my divorce (approximately 1979–85) was far more capable than the woman I had ever dreamed of being. People mentored and supported my career success and even encouraged me to look for a new relationship. I learned and grew rapidly.

But was I ready for a real relationship? Apparently not—but then apparently so. Yo-yo! After my divorce, I discovered what it felt like to be free for the first time in my life. I had some money; I had talent; I cherished the challenge of becoming the woman I wanted to be, and I wanted to be present for my children in any way I could be.

During those in-between years, relationships with men came and went—my focus was on my career and on helping to support my children. Within those few short years, I rose to higher and higher levels of executive positions, managing millions of dollars of real estate. (Millions was a lot of money back in the early 1980s.) Tom expected that he was marrying *that* woman…so did I. We were both wrong; my old root system still had longer legs than my new one.

Therefore, whenever there was conflict and I felt like I had to choose between acting on my own behalf and relinquishing that in order to please my husband, I would leave; I felt caught between two worlds. Tom was too strong and convincing; if I followed his ideas, I felt myself disappearing, and it terrified me.

As the years passed, my yo-yoing and my need to change Tom did not diminish. It helped that I traveled nationally so that our issues were not in front of us constantly. But when Tom and I were both at home, these issues would often come up the minute I walked in the door and set my suitcases down.

Life was already challenging financially. Blending our weekend families brought out the worst in both of us; our children bonded with one another much better than we bonded with each other's children. What we both learned was that if either of us attempted to make our partner choose between our marriage and our children, blood was thicker, and our relationship would be over. (Financial stress and blending families are two of the primary reasons second marriages fail.)

It was lonely and hard for both of us. That's when we went for counseling and even separated for three months. But we kept coming back to each other because there was a remarkable bond that held us fast.

Our lives and financial circumstances improved over the years, and in late 2007 Tom and I moved into the customized home of our dreams. Most of our five children were married and producing brilliant grandchildren. Tom's engineering business was doing well, and I owned a successful business as a consultant to the affordable-housing industry at a national level, which allowed me to earn what (tragically) only 3 percent of women in the United States were paid in those days. I drove an Audi TT Roadster and had been writing fiction for eight years in my "spare time." My consulting business took me around the country, where my seminars were in high demand. Somehow, I had become a success by all standards except my own.

And I was exhausted.

MARCH 26, 2008

I was awakened to a phone call from my brother that my older sister had passed away after a two-year struggle with Lou Gehrig's disease. This was the sister who had taught me to read, had kept us together as a family all the years of her life, and had expected more from life on earth than it could deliver—who either sparkled with wit and charm or doubled over with the pain of disappointment. In the end, she was unable to speak, write, walk, or function in any physical way, but she never lost her ability to smile.

APRIL 17, 2008

Death of a family member can cause seismic changes in family relationships.

After twenty-two years of marriage, I was pretty sure the best thing to do was to leave for good. I had suffered panic and anxiety for years, trying to keep everything together: my marriage, my family, my business, and my financial life. I had traveled nationwide, teaching tax regulations for eight hours a day until my body no longer knew what time it was; I couldn't sleep.

Five years earlier, I had been diagnosed with circadian-rhythm dysfunction. The key feature of circadian-rhythm disorders is a continuous or occasional disruption of sleep patterns. Medical science is learning just how important a body's circadian rhythm (twenty-four-hour sleep/awake cycle) is. If it fails, various symptoms—even diseases—appear. I learned firsthand that not being able to sleep was dangerous to my health.

It would take me weeks to heal, mostly without the loving support of my husband, who insisted that I was not having a real experience and that I needed to behave like the strong woman he knew I was. Once again we were in counseling, and my yo-yo was in play.

I'll never forget a particular marriage-therapy session in which our counselor had us stand and face each other with instructions that we were to put our palms together and then each work to get to the opposite wall. My first reaction was that I would have to fight Tom to get to my wall. He was stronger than I was, so I felt at a disadvantage. Imagine my surprise when he simply dropped his hands from mine and walked to his wall. Very telling. Like, "I can get to my goal without you, little wife." Yep, I was ready to make a break on that early spring day, just weeks after my sister had died. I had no idea that Life was ready to have a conversation with me that would change everything and lead to writing a romantic comedy that would underscore what I needed to learn.

Three

April 17, 2008: The Day the Yo-Yo Stopped (Learning THIS One Thing That Changed Everything)!

To be a true explorer is to carry on your exploration, even if it takes you to a place you didn't particularly plan to go.

—Lynne McTaggert[12]

My relationship with Tom was fragile; it didn't take much at all for me to finally snap—just a final incident in which Tom yelled at me, scolding me as if I were a stupid child. (He won't remember the incident, but I do—I kept a journal.) I'll share the incident and leave you to your own opinion.

I was trying to be helpful. Tom needed a piece of paper to write something down, and I saw such an item, along with a pen, in the pocket of his shirt. I reached for them, put the paper up against the wall, and began to write down what he needed.

Tom flew into a rage. He yelled at me in a loud, angry voice. "You know better than to do that!"

Do what? I thought to myself, completely stunned by his outburst. Then I realized that he objected to me putting the paper against the wall. I couldn't believe it—such an innocent and helpful action on my part was being angrily and harshly judged. OK, I got that the wall had been painted only a few weeks ago, but it was dry, and the paper was thick, like business-card stock. It wasn't the first time Tom had reacted to something I was doing by scolding me. In my opinion, it would be the last.

The straw landed on the camel's back. Snap. It was the end for me.

I stomped off down the hallway of our gorgeous custom home to leave for good. Tom had no idea I had planned to do that until he read this book because *I didn't leave*—ever again. In fact, that was the very day I put my yo-yo away for good—after my chat with Life about THIS.

My Conversation with Life

I've been writing fiction for over fifteen years; it's normal for me to hear characters and their conversations in my head. But that day, the dialogue wasn't between characters—it was between Life and me. It went something like this:

"Vivian, hello. That conversation you just had with your husband? It shouldn't shock you. In fact, it should sound *quite* familiar; it happens inside you all the time. You know, of course, that what just happened was that your husband was simply doing all that he could in your world—he was reflecting you."

That at least got me to stop and pay attention. "Um, I'm not sure I understand. Can you explain, please?" I asked. I remember how shocked I was.

"Think about it—do you ever speak to yourself in that horrible, scolding, and disrespectful tone of voice you just heard your husband use?"

I hesitated—I didn't spend a lot of time listening to myself talk to myself. But it hit home. "Well, OK, sure," I said. I knew I wasn't nice to myself most of the time. Most of the time a voice inside me scolded me about everything I did, no matter how good my intentions were. I didn't know how to stop it, so I had learned to ignore it.

"But that doesn't give him an excuse—" I protested.

Life had the audacity to interrupt me. "You know that nothing can show up in your life unless you attract it?"

I did; I was (and am) an avid student of the Law of Attraction and quantum physics[13]—not that I understand the science. Niels Bohr, a Danish physicist and Nobel Prize winner in atomic structure and quantum theory, is credited with saying, "Anyone who is not shocked by (quantum) physics does not understand it" ((Bohr)1999).[14]

"Well, yes," I said, "but that doesn't give him an excuse to treat me like that, and frankly, I'm tired of it. I deserve to be treated with respect."

"You certainly do. Want this conflict between the two of you to stop?"

"Absolutely. That's why I'm leaving."

"Aren't you tired of leaving your husband when he treats you like that?"

"I certainly am," I admitted.

"OK. Here's what we want you to know…what just happened *isn't about your husband*; it's about *you* and how you treat *yourself*."

Mon Dieu! I was stunned. Could this be true? I knew I was at least unkind to myself. I'd been through enough counseling to know that nearly every waking minute that I wasn't busy with something else, I was surveying my life, looking for what I was doing wrong.

"OK, I'm listening," I said, "but my husband needs to apologize for how he treated me. I'm not going to take it anymore."

"Yes, we know. But please take a moment to consider THIS, because you won't ever be tempted to leave again if you understand it: *Since nothing can show up in your world unless you attract it, could it be that your husband is treating you this way as a reflection of how you treat yourself? We call it the Law of Reflection, or LOR.*"

"Don't you mean the Law of Attraction?" I asked. *How dare I try to correct a higher power!*

"Similar," came the tender answer. "However, you can't attract anything that doesn't already exist vibrationally inside you, and that's where your efforts with the Law of Attraction are failing. You can't attract to yourself what you cannot tolerate, and right now, you can't bear a loving relationship because it violates what you believe you are worthy of. The Law of Attraction is an *external* concept that allows you to visualize what you want and to bring it to you with your thoughts.

"The Law of Reflection is an *internal* concept that allows you to take care of your internal world so that it can accept the goodness you are trying to attract. It goes deeper and gets to the root of the problem by using the external world to show you what's going on *inside* you that determines what you can and cannot attract. Do you understand the difference? You can affirm and visualize and imagine what you want for the rest of your life, but if there's an inner responder yelling, 'No, you can't; you don't deserve it,' that has to be taken care of first. How do you know you have that type of negative attitude inside you? Often the only way for you to see it is if it shows up externally like it just did in your husband's response to you.

"You know this from your years of studying quantum physics, yes? In essence you are attracting Tom's *reflection* of anger, which really isn't his at all—it's yours. It's how you treat yourself on the inside, which is the real world. You should sit down."

I did, I remember, on the end of the guest-room bed. I had read Byron Katie's book *Loving What Is*[15] a number of years earlier; I was aware that the ugliness I thought I saw coming to me from other people was really probably coming from inside me. I had not, however, had such a graphic example and such clarity as I was receiving at that precise moment.

Still, I was aghast. "You're saying Tom shouldn't apologize because how he treated me just now was really me doing it to myself? You want me to let him off the hook?"

"Not exactly. You made yourself clear to Tom, which is important. But understand that Tom was actually reflecting *you*, Vivian. He was showing you how you treat yourself on the inside of your life. Not very pretty, is it?

Since it's *your* world that you're creating, he can't bring you anything outside of your Vibrational Permission Zone, which we will call the VPZ. You can try to attract the loving husband that Tom can be, but when you are critical and harsh with yourself, that's all he can reflect. It's the way the real world works."

Vibrational Permission Zone? I'd never heard of such a thing, but it made sense.[16] I had worked with the Law of Attraction for years without much success. It's not that the Law of Attraction only works sometimes—it's that what I thought I wanted to attract and what showed up were usually quite different (and disappointing). *Could the Law of Reflection change that?*

The Law of Attraction is about how closely one's energetic focus resonates with what he or she desires. I was fairly good at attracting some of what I wanted in life, except that almost everything that showed up came to me through hard work. Plus, most of the time, once I achieved a goal, something disappointing would offset it as if I had to be punished for success. (Like the time I received an unexpected commission check of thousands of dollars and immediately fell down the stairs, double-breaking an ankle. Guess where my thousands of dollars ended up? I mean, I'm glad I had the extra cash, but you might think I would have chosen to do something different with it, yes?)

The Vibrational Permission Zone made a little sense to me: there was a low ceiling on my ability to attract what I desired without negative consequences because my inner world wasn't giving me permission. I still wasn't ready to let Tom off the hook.

"So none of this is his fault?" I still needed clarification; certainly he was partly to blame.

"Who said anything about fault?" Whoever I was talking to was obviously not a fan of my favorite activity—the blame game.

"Do you blame a mirror for what you see in it?" I was asked.

"No, of course not." I had to smile at the thought of seeing something I didn't like in the mirror and yelling at a piece of glass in my loudest shriek, "This is your fault!"

"So what you see in a mirror wouldn't be the mirror's fault, would it?"

"No. Of course not," I said again. I was sort of rolling my inner eyes but smiling at the same time. I find that Life can be witty while it's working with you.

"It would be good for you to know that your intimate partner is the most accurate reflection of your inner world. That's what we want you to understand. Do you see?"

"I suppose it's possible, but that doesn't make it OK," I said, grumbling. "I'm hard enough on myself; I don't need him to make it worse"

"Exactly! We agree. If the most important world you live in is the world within--(and that's the way it is, whether you agree or not) -- then can you see that you are creating your external world from the inside out?"

I was a staunch believer in what little I thought I understood about this core principle of quantum physics.[17] I had been studying that concept for several years. "OK, yes," I agreed

"Good because that's exactly what's going on. The good news is that if you want to fix your relationship with Tom, all you have to do is take care of what's going on in your inner world. It's not about Tom treating you badly; it's about *you* treating yourself badly. It's the Law of Reflection, and it's time for you to take it seriously if you want a different experience of life." Boy, did I!

I was instructed to go into the bathroom and look at myself in the mirror.

"Do you know what you look like?"

"Yes, of course," I said. I couldn't believe that the intelligent energy that I assumed was speaking to me would ask such an inane question but I kept my mouth shut.

"How?"

"I can see myself in the mirror." This felt pretty foolish.

"If there were no mirror and no possible way to see your reflection, would you know what you looked like?"

"I don't think so," I said. "No." I couldn't imagine not knowing what I looked like!

"OK," the voice went on. "We are applying the same principle to what just happened between you and Tom. Since your husband is your most accurate mirror—and spouses usually are, by the way—did you know that's the real reason you are attracted to each other? —he has just shown you something about your inner world. When you start treating yourself with love and respect, so will he—he has to."

"Can't he go first and show me love and respect, regardless of what's going on inside me?" I asked. "Shouldn't he show me love regardless of how I feel about myself?"

There was a smile in the reply. "He's tried that. Your VPZ won't allow it in, and your psyche can't accept it. It's like when the natives of North America couldn't see the ships of the first visitors from other continents. They had no experience with ships as visually possible, so they actually couldn't see them.

"The same is true for you—you can't see anything that's outside of your VPZ, so you don't let it in. What we'd like to suggest is that you focus on what's going on inside your own inner world and improve it. That's how you'll see the external results you desire." There was a pause—then, "Why not try it—since it works all the time?"

Did I hear a hint of fun in that dialogue?

That's when the Law of Reflection, or what I call THIS—This One Thing That Changes Everything—became real for me, and I began the most extraordinary adventure of my life. From that moment it began to change my relationship with my husband. There was more to come, but everything I needed to know was already present. That's how the universe works—it provides clarity even before our brains can process it! And it only took a couple of minutes!

In plain English, if a mirror shows me that I have a big red zit on the end of my nose, do I blame the mirror? Do I say, "You stupid mirror! How dare you?" Of course not. The mirror is doing what a mirror does. It shows me that I have a pimple so that I can take care of it—not so that it can piss me off.

Same thing with THIS. Often, the only way I become aware of something that needs attention on the inside of my life is when I see it as a reflection in my external world, and Tom is a wonderful reflector. All that's left, then, is for me to recognize it and allow it to transform. *How do I do that?* I wondered.

Life would answer that question in a few minutes.

I sat quietly and pondered what my inner self-talk actually sounded like. I would have to take care of the brutal and unforgiving voices in my head; the judging, merciless critics; and the nitpicky detailers with caustic attitudes. *Where had they come from? How could I be so hurtful to myself? Yet how could I break a lifelong habit?*

What I refer to as THIS, Dr. David Richo, PhD, a psychotherapist and author of *When the Past is Present*, calls transference. He describes transference as occasions when "feelings and beliefs from the past reemerge in our present relationships"[18] That is exactly what I'm talking about here. Until finding his book, I didn't realize there was a psychological term for it or that books had been written about what I was experiencing!

He goes on to say, "Transference is a crude way of seeing what is invisible, the untold drama inside us" (yes! yes! yes!) before he hits us with, "No one escapes transference."

Aha! Life was trying to show me something that had started long ago. It was time to go inside and heal my self-abusive attitude. But how? I didn't have to wait long for the answer. It was as if the universe was saying, "We thought you'd never ask!"

Four

How THIS Transformed My Marriage!

Each event, each person in our lives, embodies an
energetic fragment of our own psyche and soul.[19]

—Dr. David Richo

The interview with Life wasn't over. It was still April 17th, only moments since this conversation had begun. While Tom was on his way up north, I was sitting on the bed, talking to the universe! You can think I'm crazy, schizophrenic, or on some kind of illegal drug—I mean, I would if I were you—but I'm not.

Imagine my surprise after the first part of the conversation with Life had ended—the enormous clarity about why my husband was being intolerable. Now I knew, working from an understanding of the LOR, that I found my own self intolerable. THIS was quite a revelation! I got that part. Now, all I needed was the solution. It's one thing to get the insight; it's quite another to know what to do about it.

*B*ingo! Life whirled me into another reality. I knew where I was—this had to be a visual introduction to my inner world, that place I call Planet Me. (I'm pretty sure each of us has our own universe and that it pays to visit once in a while.)

"Hello. Anybody home in there?" I wandered around in a heavily timbered forest, wondering what to do next. I didn't see any goblins or monsters—no cannibals preparing a pot of stew with me as the main ingredient. Actually, I didn't see any creatures at all; it was quite peaceful, which bothered me. I knew I was here to find a way to fix my relationship with myself, and it was too darn quiet.

Eventually I stumbled into a more open and barren area, where there were no trees and very little vegetation. The landscape change was sudden and troubling. Tufts of crabgrass sprouted here and there, and weeds—only those that could survive in an obviously hostile environment—were sort of clumped together as if they needed one another for survival but weren't happy about it.

With my focus now engaged in the sudden change of terrain, I hardly noticed a monstrous, creepy old building until I almost collided with it. Looking up, I saw a kind of haunted and cobwebby mansion, complete with broken windows and missing steps to the entrance—a building one would expect to see in a horror movie.

It looked like a living thing, breathing and watching my every move, ready to devour me if I entered. It was so foreboding—I knew that no one in his or her right mind would enter it alone. Then I had to smile. *I wasn't in my right mind—I was in my inner world.* Somehow I had created this—the fact that I wanted to leave only drove me to stay.

It was the kind of place you walk into very slowly, expecting to be accosted any second. I tested the floorboards and swept my arms out in front of me to clear cobwebs and to hopefully protect myself from bats or, God forbid, any larger predators.

Suddenly a raggedly clothed, dirty, and gaunt-faced being with large, sad eyes peeked out from a room near where I was standing. (It looked something like a child, but I knew it wasn't real.) When it saw me look at it, it screamed bloody murder in an irritating high-pitched squeal. I jumped, and it took off running. Something told me to stay where I was and try to speak to it in a soothing voice. I knew my inner world was not accustomed to visitors, but I hadn't seen any No Trespassing signs. (It was my planet, so in an ethereal way, I was on my own property.)

"Hello? Anyone home? I'm Vivian Probst—I think you know me. I only want to know who you are; please don't be frightened."

"Too late!" My skin crawled at the sounds of another tortured voice.

"Yeah, too late!" an entire chorus said. I covered my ears to limit the effect of the sound. Then silence.

"I won't hurt you. I promise," I said again, uncovering my ears. I couldn't imagine what I'd done to these creatures. I thought *I* was the one who was tormented. "Maybe I can even help you," I added, hoping to tempt one of them to pay me a visit.

I cleared a place to sit down and wait, grimacing as I brushed dirt and grime away from the floorboards around me into gaping cracks and crevices. Someone needed to call in the maintenance team. Then I realized that it would probably be my job to do any cleanup.

Suddenly the little squirt I had seen earlier was standing right next to me. I jumped again.

"You promise you won't hurt me?" the strange little being asked in that high, ear-piercing voice. "Please. Please don't scold me."

"Of course not!" I said, trying to be soothing. This was difficult because of my physical reaction to its voice. "I just want to know who you are and how I can help you."

"No, you don't!" it said at the top of its lungs (although I wasn't quite sure if it had a human anatomy). I had to cover my ears again, but I could hear every word. "You only know how to make us suffer! I know who you are, even if I've never seen you. You're mean! You scold and punish me—all of us—all the time!" Then the poor little thing started weeping. Its tears created skin-colored tracks down its dirty cheeks. What could I do but invite it to sit on my lap and put my arms around it, even though it was filthy and probably had lice or worse?

"Us?" I asked. "Are there many little ones like you living here?" The weeping childlike creature only nodded. I tentatively patted its head of matted, straggly hair. It felt like fake, plastic hair such as a doll would have.

When I looked up, I saw more sad-eyed, unkempt little ones peeking out of their rooms and eyeing me cautiously. There were too many to count, and all were sobbing together.

"Who are you?" I asked.

"We are all ass-specks of yourself that you have refused to accept," my little spokesperson said. "We are your or-fans."

I hardly knew what to do or say, but I loved that it split words. I felt very much at home, since I did that all the time. It also affirmed that I was, indeed, inside my inner world and not someone else's. Life is very specific on our behalf.

"This is my first visit," I said. "I never knew a place like this existed inside me—that any of you were part of me."

"Yeah, no kidding," came its bitter reply. "You've never been here. It's about time—not that we trust you. We all have scars from where you separated us from yourself, like you wanted no-thing to do with us. Let me show you."

I didn't want to look, but I had to. When this little one lifted its shirt, I could see a gaping hole where its heart should have been. A cord was handing unattached where it obviously was intended to be plugged in to something. "See, normally this cord is attached to your heart right here." The child showed me a place on my spine, right behind my heart, a spot that had troubled me for years.

"But you closed up your heart, which cut us off. We don't get to die, so our pain never goes away. We have to wait until we're reconnected—which could be not ever."

"But here I am," I said softly. Suddenly I knew what to do.

"Hey," I said to the bundle of dirt sitting on my lap, "there's a place I'd like you to visit with me. Want to come along?" I knew there had to be some place on Planet Me that was still lovely and fun.

"Out-side? You want me to go out-side?" Its voice cut into my ears with a shriek. All the tiny ones hovering around us disappeared with the same squealing. "Outside" was obviously not a friendly place.

"We never go out-side! It's scary enough in here! Please don't make me!" My little friend practically clawed its way off my lap to escape.

"How about if I carry you in my arms and promise not to let anything hurt you? Then would you come with me?"

The eyes of this small being showed its terror and suspicion. "Why should I trust *you*? *You've* always tormented us. Why should I go anywhere with you?"

"Because I'm here," I said softly. "Because I've never actually come here before and because I think it's time for me to learn to be kinder and more loving. And I'd like to help you. Will you help me?"

The childlike creature nodded a tiny yes and snuggled back into my arms. All the other tiny heads were sticking out into the hallway, listening.

"OK," I said, "I think there's a place where we can have some fun together. Let's go find it!" I stood up carefully. I hoped wherever we ended up, it would have a tub or shower.

"What is *fun*?"

That did it. My heart seized up, and I wept. I knew that for every one of these orphans on Planet Me, life was anything but fun. I was unloving, critical, and always finding ways to punish them (myself) for not being perfect. I didn't know why I was that way, and now that I could see the impact, it bothered me. *What could I do to change that?*

"I think you'll like it. I'll show you," I said. "And you don't need to be afraid—any of you."

"OK. But don't you dare hurt me, or none of us will ever allow you to visit here again."

I figured this little band of tortured orphans wouldn't be able to prevent me from touring my own inner world, but I had to admire their bravado. Then I thought of *Gulliver's Travels* and decided it best not to assume that just because these beings were small, they were weak.

As I stepped outside, cradling my dirtball friend, the other little ones gathered around the door, careful not to leave the building. It was obvious from the forlorn looks on their faces that they were sure they would never see their friend again.

What I needed was a safe and magical place to show this sad piece of myself how to be happy and have fun.

"*H*ey, what's your name?" I suddenly wanted to know.

"I am called One," came the reply. "My full name is Wrong One. There are hundreds of us, so we just use numbers."

Hundreds? My heart sank.

"You may not know it, but you've got serious overcrowding going on here. There isn't enough room for all of us. We don't expect you to be concerned on *our* behalf, but you should be very concerned for yourself."

"Why is that?" I was curious, not concerned.

"Because when none of us can leave, we get very, very mean—in case you haven't noticed."

I cleared my throat. "How do you mean that?" I thought a little play on words would lighten the mood.

"You can't see it, can you?"

"See what?" Now I was more than curious.

"You can't see that unless you take care of your problems, it's *you* who suffers."

What could I say?

"Have you noticed that other people are becoming more negative around you?"

"Are you saying it's my fault? I just think the world is so full of such horrors that none of us can help but be tainted by it." I wanted to explain why it was so easy for me to get down in the dumps.

"A wise man once said, 'You get world peace through inner peace. If you've got a world of people who have inner peace, then you have a peaceful world.'"[20]

"How would you know something like that, locked away in my inner world?" I asked.

"Plenty of time to study," my little smart aleck replied.

"OK, I give. Who's the wise man?" I asked.

"Wayne Dyer. Ever heard of him?"

"Of course. You would know that."

"You could take what you read more seriously. It might help with the overcrowding."

I carried Wrong One in my arms until quite magically we came to the edge of a pool of pink, sparkling energy. There was even a waterfall of the same substance above it, creating a sense of wonder and beauty as it poured over the edge and into the pool below. As the energy from the waterfall splashed to the pool, it created multiple rainbows of the most incredible colors. I knew what I was seeing had to be love as it appeared on my planet. WOW! Hopefully it was unconditional love with a magical cleaning cycle. Number One could use a bath.

"One! Just look at that!" I squealed with delight.

One shrank deeper into my arms, greatly alarmed. "Are you going to make me go in there? Is it going to hurt? I am so tired of being in pain. Please tell me you didn't bring me here to cause me to suffer more! What about my heart string? What if it falls off?"

"OK," I said. "Sit here and watch me. Then if you want to try it, we'll do it together, OK? If you don't, that's OK, too. We can always go back any time you want to." One gulped and nodded. "And I'll take care of your heart string so it doesn't get damaged."

I took a step into the pool and instantly felt the awesome power of love begin to course through me. I turned to One and smiled. "See, I'm fine. In fact, I'm wonderful!" I laughed and splashed around.

One giggled and then stopped in surprise. "What was that noise I just made? You're a different color than you were before."

"That noise was laughter," I said. "You were having fun."

Looking down at myself, I saw that One was right; my entire being had turned pink. "It feels wonderful!" I exclaimed, even though I understood that my little friend had no idea what *wonderful* was. I had not felt like this in so long!

Next, I swam to the waterfall and let it pour over my metaphorical head and body.

One giggled. "You look ridiculous."

"Well," I said, "looking ridiculous is fun! Want to try it?" I came out of the pool and offered One my hand.

"OK, but I'm scared. Can you carry me?" One reached up to me, causing tears to once again gather in my eyes.

"Of course I can," I said. "I would love to."

And so I did. I gathered up that orphan part of myself that had long been forgotten and neglected. I vowed never to let go. When I was waist deep in the pool of love, I said, "Give me your hand, One."

I took that hand, and together we touched the pink energy flowing in the pool.

"That's nice!" One squealed, laughing again. "I want to jump in! Will you catch me?"

"Of course," I said, smiling. "This is what fun feels like, One."

"I think we should share this with the others," One said thoughtfully. "It could help with the overcrowding."

We played there for what seemed like hours until I felt the energy of One begin to bond with me. Suddenly we were not separate—we were together again. I would not be taking One back to the Orphanage as a separate, detached part of me. I hoped the others would notice that we were reunited and would want to join me as well.

It was clear that I would be making a lot of visits to this magical place. Whenever I felt hurt, sorrow, pain, or regret—especially if Tom showed it to me—I knew I would visit the Orphanage to find my wounded vibrational match and heal it back into love. In this way, I could live my whole life with all of me put back together.

One taught me that by not dealing with my old feelings, every new hurt only added itself on top of everything else. Carrying such a load without consequence was almost impossible. Maybe that was why I felt so heavyhearted so much of the time. Aha!

*T*he story ended there. Immediately I began to pay more attention to what was going on inside me than outside. THIS is the process by which Life helped me overcome years of hurt and trauma that probably occurred earlier than my memory was able to recall—perhaps even prior lifetimes. I would never need to leave Tom again! And I no longer had to wonder what "technique" to use to heal any suffering that showed up in my external world. Life had given me a visual. The message was crystal clear—as clear as the pool of loving energy that I now visit whenever a feeling that needs my attention shows up.

Through Tom's ability to reflect my inner world back to me, I learned what was going on inside of me with incredible precision. I experimented with THIS for days, weeks, and months until it became a natural part of my life. In the early days, I remember scrutinizing everything Tom did or said to me or about me—how he treated me. It became a fascinating game.

If there was discord with Tom, I used it as a signal to immediately go inside myself to find the vibrational match, which was always waiting for me at the Orphanage. What happened was that Tom and I found ourselves truly enjoying our marriage. For me, it was immensely liberating to no longer look at my husband as someone to blame or as someone who had to change in order for me to be happy. In time, I learned that I didn't have to wait for Tom to reflect something for me. Sensitive to my own inner world, I learned to apply THIS to whatever needed attention, and issues disappeared. It didn't matter where they started or how old they were. Everything, no matter what it was (or is, as I am still practicing and learning), transformed when I took it through THIS process.

Whether it's Fred Alan Wolf or the group of entities known as Abraham; whether it's Neale Donald Walsch or Rumi; or whether it's Dr. David Richo or Byron Katie, Louise Hay, Wayne Dyer, or Deepak Chopra, I have found great clarity in the teachings of others. In fact, as I was writing this chapter, a quote from Abraham came across my computer saying, *"You don't have to go back and deal with childhood issues, because those childhood issues produced a vibration within you that you are still offering—which is producing today's issues. You can shift your vibration a whole lot easier when you're dealing with today's issues, than trying to deal with childhood issues. It's the same vibration. That vibration that was creating childhood issues—now it's creating today issues. Deal with it in your now."²¹* Perfect.

Regardless of what we call the unresolved issues in our lives, they are only there because we have work to do before they can leave, and I, at last, decided not to hold my husband accountable for the problems that were showing up for me. That's what visiting my Inner Orphanage taught me.

Five

May 17th, 2008: Why I Had to Write *Death by Roses*

In which Mae Rose McElroy dies on the toilet after a final fit of rage at her husband, goes into her afterlife and finds out 'it could have been a wonderful life!'

- Vivian Probst

I t was still 2008 and just one month since Life had taught me the concept of THIS. May 17th, began as a normal day. I was working on finishing the fifth volume in a fictional series titled "(The Woman Who Forgot Who She Was". I have not touched it since that day when the story that became "Death by Roses" pushed its way into my soul. How was I to know that this new romantic comedy would be my foray into becoming a published author and that it would use humor and sass to make sure I understood the concept of THIS?

If you work intuitively, as I do, you know all about the voice that talks to you about a new idea; you know how emphatic it can be, driving you almost out of your mind until you agree to take on whatever it's impressing on you. I also know what it's like to try to disregard it. It's not like we *have to* do what is being suggested—it's just that if we don't, I'm convinced that we birth a regret.

When the immense energy of a very large woman (I mean, she filled the entire Double-French doorway of my home-writing studio) showed up and said, "Here, honey, write this," who was I to refuse?

In his book *On Writing*, Steven King, a man who knows about writing fiction, says,

> Good story ideas seem to come quite literally from nowhere, sailing at you right out of the empty sky...your job isn't to find these ideas but to recognize them when they show up...I believe plotting and the spontaneity of real creation aren't compatible. It's best that I be as clear about this as I can—I want you to understand that my basic belief about the making of stories is that they pretty much make themselves. The job of the writer is to give them a place to grow. My job... [is] to watch what happens and write it down. That's exactly my experience. Therefore, when the energy that put these ideas together in my head showed up with instructions, I listened. [22]

It's hard to say why *Death by Roses* came to me when and as it did, but I spent the next five years watching and listening to the characters in the story *while my husband's voice could be heard faintly in the background, saying, "Publish the damn book!"*

None of my stories had ever been published in any traditional way. Therefore, it was a miracle when, "quite by accident" (or due to the bellowing of my husband), I found the When Words Count Retreat[23] in Vermont where I could work with their team to make my novel contest-worthy. *Death by Roses* went on to win a New York publishing award specifically created for new authors. It took a couple of years to polish the story and a year to get it printed. By that time, I was sold on THIS, not only for my marriage, but for my life.

As I began to tour bookstores and visit with book clubs, it finally dawned on me that *Death by Roses* was a fictional framework for THIS! What fun!

Not surprisingly, it's the tale of the unhappy marriage of whipped, long-suffering Art McElroy and his bossy wife, Mae Rose. Their thirty-year marriage ends abruptly after Mae Rose directs a (final) fit of rage at her husband (for what she believes is a good reason) and stomps off to the bathroom, suffers a heart attack, and dies right on the toilet. (Check out the book's cover someday soon!)

During her "Reflection" in higher realms, Mae Rose learns the truth about the incident that killed her and, even more importantly, that *she and Art could have had a wonderful life together.*

I think you're going to love "The Dial" in the story. It's a tool Mae Rose uses in her afterlife to review her life on earth and to see how much better (or worse) it could have been. She didn't realize that she could have used "The Dial" while she was living, but I took the hint from her and started using mine right away. Thank you fictional May Rose McElroy for sharing this idea! Personally, I was thrilled that the story was given to me so that I could "dial up" a wonderful life and marriage while Tom and I are still earthbound.

Meanwhile, on earth, her widowed husband, Art, is going through his own discoveries along the same lines—realizing he could have appreciated his wife a whole lot more and probably could have avoided having the affair that drove them apart.

In her determination to reconcile with Art, Mae Rose decides to violate the only rule in heaven: no meddling! That little violation will land her in a hilariously outrageous form of "hell on earth"—inside the dying body of a female horror-film producer. It's worth a read just for fun, and it's chock full of the wisdom of THIS.

For those of us who have a propensity to blame others for our unhappiness, *Death by Roses* suggests that there might be a (much) better way. During the years I was writing the story, I practiced THIS right alongside the principles I was laughing my way through while writing. Our marriage continued to flourish more and more.

You might notice that Mae Rose becomes defensive as she initially goes through her afterlife Reflection (which is a lot like Judgment Day but much more fun). First, she tries to tell her agent that she's not supposed to be dead. That doesn't help.

Then she suggests that God wasn't all that clear about how to have a happy marriage—that perhaps "someone" had failed her and hadn't explained it well enough while she was on earth. Poor Mae Rose—she is informed that she was too busy dissing her husband to ever hear what God was trying to tell her.

Ouch! That part of the story was getting personal. But just like Mae Rose, I went through a phase in which I argued about THIS. It seemed to me that Life was saying that any problems in my life were *my* fault, until I saw the difference between fault and responsibility, which are very different concepts, as will come to light below. Fault is married to blame and creates guilt; responsibility and awareness are also partners. Their union creates love. I had to pick who I was going to live with. Was the choice really all that difficult?

Six

WHAT? I'M SUPPOSED TO STOP BLAMING MY SPOUSE? ARE YOU CRAZY?

*I never knew that taking full responsibility
for my life could be so much fun!*

- VIVIAN PROBST

Mae Rose was an award-winning blamer. If there were trophies given, she'd have had a wall full. One of the problems with "the blame game" is that we teach it to others, especially our children.

My maternal ancestors would roll over in their graves if they caught me confessing to letting go of one of the most basic survival tools of our subservient lives. Blame kept us alive—it allowed us to feel equal, even if our religion said we weren't. After all, didn't most of our stories about blame start with the classic events as told in the Bible about Adam and Eve? Mostly Eve, yes?

My growing-up mantra was one of blame. (Watch how the word splits: b-lame; b-lame-me). There were four of us children under the age of six. We were very good at blaming one another when Mom lined us up for an interrogation. But Mom was good at it, too.

Blame was big in our religion. The devil, our sinful natures, the carnal world—all were constantly tempting us to go astray. In the very evangelical (or 'eve-angelic-al' in my linguistic mind. Such a word split would grant Eve and the angels a little more credit than they normally receive in the conservative Christian culture in which I grew up). Women were appreciated to a certain degree but held no authoritative positions. Because of Mother Eve's grievous encounter with that tempting serpent in the Garden of Eden (and because the Apostle Paul declared it to be so), women were considered much more inclined toward sin—and to tempt men toward sin. Therefore, we had to be watched. Obedience to the (less sinful) male was a serious aspect of funda-mental Christianity. The word 'fundamental is another interesting word split: fun-da-men-tal). It was *not* fun for women; men have always held a higher position). Somehow, even after all these years, many people still believe that (a) God is a man and (b) that men are closer to God because Mother Eve took the first bite of the fruit.

*B*lame was an important coping mechanism for women in my childhood culture. I learned from my female ancestors how to artfully circumvent our reduced status by undertaking the task of reminding men that they had their own issues—that they weren't perfect. I was trained to see what was wrong with men, how to deal with them, and how to keep them in line. ("If a man speaks in a forest, is he still wrong?")

"Oh, if only your father would change!" is a lament I often heard from my mother.

I learned all the ways to survive the reduced status of being a woman in a religion that didn't put us at the head of the class. We weren't permitted to be express negative emotions; in fact, we weren't allowed to have them at all. Somehow we adapted, creatively. Some of us used the "poor me" suffer-ing mantra with a lot of sighing, which I call the "martyr effect." Some of us painted happy smiles on our faces so that no one knew our pain, aka the "silent-suffering effect." The internal damage was horrible.

Those who couldn't suffer silently often became what I call "subtle spouse squeakers," talking about their relationship very quietly (but with growing malice) to other women. Or they became "imperfection-list lovers," looking for all the things about their spouses that were wrong.

Such responses were coping mechanisms for women like me whose social standing often left them seriously unhappy and craving some sort of relief. (OK, this wasn't true for all of us, but for a lot of us it was.) We talked about men; we confessed our own spiritual shortcomings in the same breath as we complained about the imperfections of the male species. It was our way of letting it be known that we weren't quite ready to bow down and worship.

It was a lot of the extra baggage to carry around—that sense of unworthiness, of reluctant obedience, of shame that required us to hide our feelings—and I knew in my soul (in that place I refused to visit) that men should not hold a higher place of authority just because of some genital differences. While I conformed to the standard set by our mission leaders lest I be accused of sin, no one could convince me that I was supposed to submit just because I came into the world with a vagina instead of a penis. But it was what I was taught; I went along and behaved myself because I was afraid of what could happen if I didn't—until I couldn't any longer.

OK. Learning THIS required me to give up blame and surrender to the idea of complete responsibility for every event and occurrence in my life as a reflection of something inside me that needed my attention. I learned not to hold my spouse responsible for my happiness, and I extend the same courtesy to myself. It's not about blame; it's about awareness that allows me to act on what I see going on inside myself and to resolve it with unconditional self-love.

Can you see how the word *resolve* can be broken into two parts—re-solve—to suggest that we are solving something that has already been solved before? I take that to suggest that there's already an answer to my problem. Can you also see the word l-o-v-e inside resolve? Reorder the letters and *re-solve* becomes *re-loves*. Powerful language!

If we swim with fault and guilt in the Blame Pool of Life, we can get eaten alive. I can't help but think of the old movie, *African Queen*, and those nasty leeches that suck blood from poor Charlie as he and Rose trudge through swampland with their ruined boat. When I think of guilt, fault, and blame, I think of those leeches. Ew! I want them off right now! Are you with me? This is perfect for leech prevention.

In the Blame Pool, we swim with predators that are looking for only one thing—a way to destroy who we really are. It's not pretty—the process of rationalizing why I'm *not* responsible when things go wrong. Who would pick a cesspool of slime, judgment, and degradation over a pool of sparkling love?

So I don't want to swim there; I choose the Pool of Unconditional Love, recognizing and repairing whatever I see going on in my inner world that does not please me or reflect what I want in my life.

This is *not* about fault, guilt, or blame. It's about loving ourselves and taking responsibility to heal very old wounds that so many of us don't know we have. As we release them into love, we become free to be our true selves!

Some people hate the word *responsibility*—not that I *blame* them. But I think perhaps we don't understand what that word really means. I'd like to take you on a linguist's journey into words—at least, this linguist's trek. Watch what happens!

Let's take the word *responsibility* apart.

Response-ability.[24]

The ability to respond—that's not so scary, is it?

It's only our interpretation of the word that makes us dislike it.

If we compare our linguistic definition of *responsibility* to the dictionary, let's also then ask which feels better and gives us a sense of control.

Here's *Merriam-Webster's* online dictionary definition of responsibility:

1. The state of being the person who caused something to happen
2. A duty or task that you are required or expected to do
3. Something you should do because it is morally right, legally required, etc.
4. Burden

Ugh. That's pretty heavy, and that's where we get hung up. Which do I prefer, and which feels better? Responsibility as the "ability to respond" or the "duty"—the burden of what is morally right? It is what we decide about this word that puts our footprint on the path we choose to take.

On Planet Me, I take responsibility and cherish it! I get to choose how I am going to respond to what I see from my external world that is reflecting my inner world. Yes, sometimes I'd prefer not to—but when I get to that place and make my choice not to blame but to investigate and resolve, I feel fabulous! And, of course, the issue can vanish because I've resolved and released it into Unconditional Love.

Wherever the patterns of mistreating myself came from—whatever situations locked them into my psyche—finding a responsible 'other' party and beating them up or blaming them isn't going to change a thing. The only way to move it out of my world is to acknowledge that it exists there in the first place as evidenced by the reflection I'm seeing in my outer world. It isn't my fault that it's there, but it's my responsibility to acknowledge and to take care of it. THIS takes care of THAT.

THIS means that I want the best "reflector" I can find so that I can achieve the most positive results on Planet Me. And this means...

Seven

AHA! SO THAT'S WHY I MARRIED YOU!

Lovers don't finally meet somewhere.
They're in each other all along.[25]

- RUMI

THIS is where my relationship changed. Yes, we get married because of love, but there's another reason I discovered—a big one that I had been missing.

Could it be that I want to engage you, my intimately significant other, because *you reflect me so brilliantly*? There's just something about you…and I've come to understand THIS is what it is. You, my partner, lover, cherished companion, don't "complete" me (as the great old movie *Jerry McGuire* suggests in that passionate scene in the elevator)—*please*—you reflect me! Once I got that, everything else about what was right or wrong in my relationship with Tom disappeared quickly in the wonder of discovery.

What I've learned in my years of practicing is that THIS *brings love back and amplifies it.* In the absence of blame, there is love—deep, true love because I now understand more about what love is and how it really works.

This is the part where I have to remind you once again that I don't have a degree in relationship counseling. I'm not a licensed therapist, and there's no reason for you to believe anything I say—except that what I am sharing is supported by science and spiritual practices, and it has worked for me for years.

As I've already said, THIS is not a new concept. If you've read the King James Version of the Bible, perhaps the "mote and beam" verses (Matthew 7:3–5) will ring a bell.

"³ And why beholdest thou the mote that is in thy brother's eye, but considerest not the beam that is in thine own eye?

⁴ Or how wilt thou say to thy brother, let me pull out the mote out of thine eye; and, behold, a beam is in thine own eye?

⁵ Thou hypocrite, first cast out the beam out of thine own eye; and then shalt thou see clearly to cast out the mote out of thy brother's eye."

My version is: How dare I look at *you* as having a problem (the mote, which is an ever-so-tiny piece of something) unless I am willing to see *my* own larger problem (the beam, which is described as a large timber of wood)? Does divine love have a sense of humor or what?

Perhaps if I take care of my problem, I'll notice that yours disappears as well. That's what I know.

THE MYTH OF "THAT'S YOUR PROBLEM!"

Did you notice that *o-u-r* is three-quarters of the word '*your*'? It reminds me of the old ditty about pointing a finger at someone. Even as kids we knew that pointing at someone meant that three of our finder fingers were pointing back at us.

Suddenly, declaring something as my spouse's problem and not mine no longer made sense. It wasn't the declaration of independence or the correct assignment of responsibility I had thought it was—it couldn't be, if THIS was correct. It became much more accurate for me to observe what was going on with Tom and ask myself, *How does this reflect something inside me?*

The beauty of THIS is that both Tom and I get credit for everything wonderful coming into our lives. THIS creates unbelievable unity and companionship. Yes, things happen that tip our wonderful world upside down occasionally, but with THIS, instead of blame, there is cooperation. Instead of "Where did this come from—oh, it must be *your* fault," it's "Look at that! I wonder where that precious little orphan is on Planet Me?" I take a look, find where the problem is, and love it back into myself. It's important to note that I'm seeing the reflection of the <u>feeling</u>, not the circumstances on the outside. If I want to find the reflective quality, I have to look for that inside. *Where is that feeling of unworthiness, worry, guilt, anger or blame living inside of me?*

I'd like to add that our partners might not know or understand what we've discovered; they might not even be interested, and that's perfectly fine. Anyone can do THIS, and it doesn't take 'two to tango' when it comes to applying *THIS* to a marriage.

Tom is a scientist—a rational, logical engineer. I don't really know if he's embraced THIS the way I have and it doesn't matter. Don't set yourself up for disappointment by thinking that your life partner will embrace the wonder of what you've discovered—and frankly, it's OK if your partner doesn't. I didn't tell Tom I was studying THIS for many years, and even now that he knows, I haven't heard him tell me how much it's changed his life. THIS changed my world, and he's a visitor there, so it changes our relationship—it has to. It's my planet—I can do what I want to! Oh la la!

THE REFLECTION ATTRACTION FACTOR

This brings us right back to perhaps the biggest blind spot we have in considering our attraction to each other. Yes, it's love, *and*, I believe, it's more. I call it "The Reflection Attraction Factor." There's a part of me that understands on a level that I'm not usually conscious of that I will benefit from an intimate relationship with my mate. Our intimate relationship allows me to see aspects of myself that I otherwise will probably ignore to my own detriment.

The Reflection Attraction Factor can also work to bring the very same issue up again (and again and again), until I see it and "resolve" it. Then I watch with wonder as my partner transforms into a person I love more and more because I love myself more and more.

Once again, we can relish the ability to look back and see how Life in its infinite wisdom brought us together. Remember the circumstances that caused you and your partner to meet? What about the miracle of the two of your being created separately by the close encounter of four other people? (Yes, I know that today, technology doesn't require that we actually 'meet' the other person who will help generate life, we can do it from a test tube. But so far, it still takes two, so to speak.)

Incredibly amazing circumstances must coordinate themselves to actually create life, much less bring us together in time and space. How could I deny that Tom and I had met under miraculous circumstances? Surely it wasn't just for us to cause each other misery! I had to understand that reason, and I refused to leave until I did. Except once I did, I didn't have to leave. Oh la la!

When I stopped to reconsider what divinely orchestrated circumstances yielded my relationship with Tom, I lost my ability to argue against us. When I learned THIS, our relationship became even more sacred. If it feels like a relationship came from anywhere but divine love and light—especially then, it's important to ask these questions.

I believe we all are intentional about meeting the people we do in this lifetime, and nowhere is it more visible than in our most intimate relationships.

For instance:

I marveled when a client told me that she met her future husband over a hibachi grill in a restaurant as they were discussing a computer problem she was having. He was from LA; she was from Saint Louis. They met in Kansas City and are now married with children. How does that happen? Call it a fluke; call it luck; call it fate. Whatever we call it, it's best if we own it.

Another friend went all the way to Germany to meet a man who almost didn't get leave from his army base to meet her. Only a few hours made all the difference, and then, just in the nick of time, he got time off and they met. That was decades ago.

Or how about the woman who "ran into" an old childhood friend from Illinois at a rock concert in San Francisco years later? Really?

We can look at these examples and say, "Yes, those are very fortunate indeed, but my relationship isn't like that at all." Some of us might say, "What relationship? I don't have a story like that to tell." If we understand that it's all intended for us to have a wonderful life, it can make all the difference in the world to how we function.

If we can consider for a moment that we meet each other precisely because there is a "relationship attraction factor"—a specific reason for the two of us to find each other throughout all time and eternity, it can give us a wonderfully new perspective. There's more to why we married each other than appears on the surface. There's a deeper reason we marry the person we marry. Simply considering the wonder of it and giving thanks is enough to move forward.

Which brings us to the idea of gratitude. No matter where a relationship is at the current time, gratitude will do more than anything else to move it down the right road—even if it's time to take separate paths. Holding on to resentment keeps us stuck. With THIS we can let that go and experience the best Life has to offer us. Life stopped me from leaving my second marriage because it knew that I was running away from something that I didn't want to face about my own inner world—and that if I stayed, I could have deeper love. Thank you Life!

Eight

PSSST. YOU'VE GOT ORPHANS!
(A NEW PERSPECTIVE ON TRAUMA AND ABUSE)

*Our parents weren't holding out on us. They may not have
had as much to give as we required...Our work now is
our own: we grieve what we missed; we let go of the past;
we take full responsibility for our life in the present.*

- DR. DAVID RICHO[26]

I didn't realize that most mothers do not take their anger out on their children as they scrub their tiny heads under a faucet of water by raking their nails painfully into their children's scalps or that when I protested that the bathtub water was too hot, most mothers would add some cool water rather than saying in a demanding tone, "I said, 'Sit down!'"

Spanking was A-OK in those days, and I marvel that young children today can be raised without it. We were beaten with whatever was handy when Mom was angry—it didn't even have to be our fault. If Mom was mad because Dad couldn't spend time with her when she felt particularly upset, she would take the four of us speeding down the road in the car. We were terrified as we begged her to slow down. Telling Dad our concerns would only get us in more trouble.

Perhaps the worst abuse I felt as I grew up was my mother's need to take me into her confidence and tell me what was wrong with my father—about how unhappy she was because he wouldn't change. She could go into great detail. I didn't know what to do—so I just listened as she blamed him for everything that felt wrong to her, expecting me to understand and support her. *Really?*

Mom would sit on the phone, weeping to her best friend for hours at a time about how awful her life was; she punished her children because she was angry with her husband, and she blamed herself for not being able to fulfill their dreams of being medical missionaries. Years later they would return to missionary work. I was never convinced that my mother found the life she wanted to live there and she continued to suffer.

I was too young to know the impact of her nervous breakdown after my younger sister was born. I didn't know that electroconvulsive therapy[27] could dramatically change a person like it did my mother (although I do not remember knowing her before her treatment as I was so young). I believe we never got to know a loving mother and that all of us carried that pain into our adulthood. In fact, I had no idea what a mother's love could be like until I watched my children raising their children.

*I*f someone asks where our orphans (wounds that do not heal) come from, there are any number of counselors who will send us back to the early years of our lives, although, as Abraham[28] says, we don't really need to go back there because the vibration still lives inside of us. All we have to do is find that wound (often through THIS) and heal it with love.

I've explained how I now cope with my orphans and that it's best for me to assume that anything that shows up on Planet Me is there with my permission and as part of my creation, no matter how old it is or how long ago it occurred. Somehow these difficult experiences made it past my VPZ shields. It doesn't matter if I recognize my visitor as friend or foe; the energy I am experiencing has made it through my VPZ. Anything that crosses that threshold is mine to take care of. Period.

OK. Perhaps not everyone lives with a bunch of missing aspects of herself or himself, hiding out on the inside of his or her lives and screwing things up. But I believe many of us do, and there are probably quite a few of us who just don't know it.

Perhaps we think that since we weren't physically or sexually abused as young children, we have no orphans—no suffering, disconnected aspects of ourselves. It might be true—of course it might. But if life has its spiked heel in the middle of our backs and no matter what we do, we can't get up and get on with our lives, I believe it's safe to assume there's something keeping us on the ground. I care less about what it is than I do about recognizing that it exists and drenching it and myself with love. I want it *gone!*

I had no idea that my early childhood was traumatic until a Jungian[29] ther-apist suggested it as a possibility based on the symptoms I was experienc-ing when I was in my fifties. I was stuck in a tough place, and I couldn't get out.

According to a blog post titled "Childhood Trauma and the Mind-Body Connection for Adults"[30] (Thompson 2010), physical symptoms of early childhood trauma in adults include:

- Lack of eye contact
- Altered pattern of speech
- Exhaustion that may be chronic adrenal fatigue
- Anxiety (including panic attacks)
- Shallow breathing
- Chronic back pain
- Hypervigilance
- Feeling frozen or an inability to sit still

The blog also provides a list of the emotional symptoms as follows:

- Having trouble functioning at home or work
- Suffering from severe fear, anxiety, or depression
- Being unable to form close, satisfying relationships
- Experiencing terrifying memories, nightmares, or flashbacks
- Avoiding more and more things that remind you of the trauma

I cannot emphasize enough that THIS process is a compassionate way to bring love to these old wounds. The challenge for many of us is that we don't want to face these problems or that often our traumas are too subtle for us to recognize except as *they show up repeatedly in our outside world*. We often forget that we were tiny children when these crises developed and that those feelings, if not resolved through love, still haunt us.

No, I don't believe that all of us are intentionally traumatized by others as much as we are by our still hidden interpretation of the actions of others, even if those actions were well intended. I call these "subtle abuses" (see my list under Exhibit A at the end of this chapter), because they are almost invisible. If we weren't beaten or sexually abused—if we don't remember our childhoods as being extremely troubled—we might think we are OK and that we should be marching right along, living happy, productive lives. We don't understand why it is that we keep stumbling or hitting that brick wall. We don't even accept it when life is being good to us—because we can't stand it.

Here's an example of what I would consider a subtle abuse: a few years ago, as my therapist and I were working through my own discovery, it was my good fortune to have a friend take me into her confidence about some of her own problems. She was feeling stuck; her marriage and her career weren't working.

When I asked about her childhood, she informed me that it was perfectly wonderful and abuse-free. *Lucky you!* I thought. She assured me of this by sharing an example: "My mother would always allow me to make my own bed. Then she would unmake it and show me how to do it more correctly. She was always doing this to show me how to do things better."

What about that is not demeaning to a child? Can we see the subtlety? I thought, *OK. Here's a well-intentioned mother trying to teach her child the absolutely critical value of making her bed correctly.* (I'm joking about the "absolutely critical" part.) If I had been her daughter, I would have taken her remaking the bed practice as, "OK, honey, show me how you do it, and then I'll show you a better way. I'll always be better at this than you are."

Can we see how subtle it is? That awareness took my friend into a new place in her life. How often do we wear blindfolds in front of the mirror so that we can't see that red zit (or that trauma), because a mirror can't lie? Is it possible that we don't want to take the blindfold off?

Another example comes from a friend who laments how poorly her older sister treated her as she was growing up. That sister died almost a decade ago, yet today, in her sixth decade of life, the living sister continues to be haunted by that wound. THIS helps us heal those old injuries!

For those who get through life with great vitality and enthusiasm, able to manifest their every desire, all I can say is you probably don't need to read this part of the book. I can also say, "Lucky you," and no longer feel deep jealousy consume me. Oh, I had the same dreams and the desires that seem to be packaged inside us when we're born, but I either had a punishing parent, a religion of sin and guilt, or my sense of unworthiness fighting me every step of the way. If I succeeded at something, which I often did, I paid for it, because it just wasn't OK with my inner sense of self. I don't believe I'm the only one who has that going on. What I learned is that there's a way to move beyond that, and for me, THIS is it!

In my journey to Planet Me, as I began to encounter my many orphans, I became aware, through the assistance of a great therapist, that I, too, had experienced not-so-subtle and traumatic abuses that were affecting my adult life.

Please bear in mind that I'm not talking about abuse so that we can blame others for our trials. Living life as a victim is not charming and not worthy of the real reason we're in this life. Thinking *there's nothing I can do about what happened to me in the past, so I'll never be able to overcome my pain in the future* is being a victim and not what THIS is all about.

In truth, once I realized what was happening on Planet Me, I could then accept responsibility for resolving it.[31] I hadn't created it, perhaps, but I had clung to it and embraced it in my VPZ, probably because it was familiar and felt like comfort food to me. I didn't have to spend years trying to forgive or release what had happened—I didn't have to spend time hating those who were instrumental in bringing it to me—I just cleared it out. I will keep doing that if something else shows up.

Dear Lord, I was in my fifties when a therapist finally suggested that I had some unresolved issues, most likely from my early childhood! I hadn't considered it before because I was busy reaching for my dreams, some of which were coming true, but all of which were causing me deep despair. So much good was occurring in my life, but over the course of time, I had grown weary of reaching goals and getting my hand slapped. If I succeeded at anything, I paid for it somewhere else.

What had taken me into therapy was the need to understand *why* I could get so far and no farther and why, even with all that I had accomplished in my wonderful life, there was a cruel voice that constantly reminded me, "You're no big deal. All this doesn't mean anything. You'll see. You should just stop trying."

Funny how that sounded vaguely like my mother, who had told me when my career began to take off, "You'll find when you reach my age that none of it means anything." If that's what she believed and taught my innocent self in my early childhood, was there any wonder that the same thing was happening in my adult life? I'm very near my mother's age when she passed away, and I can say for sure that everything makes a difference! I want it all in this lifetime, and I will do what it takes to keep moving ahead.

Yes, I'd had a tough early childhood; it became clear that the punishing voices playing relentlessly in my head were those of a raging and abusive mother, a scolding and frustrated father, a religion that focused on how sinful I was, and so many other factors. But let's not get stuck there. Let's apply THIS.

I don't believe any of us get through life without issues to deal with. Dr. Richo makes it clear that all of us deal with transference—the unresolved issues from the past that uncannily show up in current relationships. Once we can see these, however, we can grow through them into our full adult lives, he explains (Richo 2008).

Of course, learning all this in my early fifties after much of my career was over was no picnic; I desperately ached to have all those years back. I wanted a do-over, just like Mae Rose in *Death by Roses*. (OK. Maybe not the type of do-over Mae Rose had, but the one she wanted—just to be clear.)

OK, Vivian, I told myself, *put your "big-girl panties" back on. You've gotten this far, and you're not going to get those years back. Let's look forward to the future.* I adopted a better-late-than-never attitude and did what I always did with a new discovery: I researched and applied and studied and implemented until I got to THIS.

There are numerous therapies for dealing with old trauma. I was lucky that my younger sister was still living and that we could support each other as we dealt with our wounds. Between the two of us, we tried pretty much everything, but for me, nothing worked like THIS. I just never imagined that Life would use my own husband to lead me to the solution I so desperately craved!

Most therapies help, of course, and many of them can cure the problem effectively. THIS is a great companion to any process, be it hypnosis, psychotherapy, past-life regression therapy, Jungian psychology (which was particularly fascinating and helpful to me, since I have fairly graphic dreams), EMDR (eye movement desensitization and reprocessing)[32], homeopathy, rebirthing, or even medication, as long as it is accompanied by therapy. For me, THIS took me to the place where I could truly heal myself through love. It was only when I took the journey to Planet Me, visited the Orphanage, and spent time splashing around with my wounds in the Pool of Unconditional Love that I was able to begin to feel free. But I had support and caring professionals to help me get there. Please remember that.

All of us are going to be hurt by life from time to time; it's inherent in a world of contrast. My purpose here is not to make us think that we are all so mistreated that we need massive amounts of therapy or that we will live lives of despair because of our histories. However, if we have some old unresolved issues (and we can know this according to how life is working for us *right now*), THIS might enable us to get to the source of the pain and become free.

Abusive patterns, intentional or not, can eventually become self-abuse when we internalize them or when they become what I call a preference for suffering. I believe it can be trained into us from before we are born if those who conceive us carry the marker and/or find themselves inconvenienced by being pregnant at the time we are womb-bound, as was my case.

I also believe it's possible that, as I look around my external world and recognize that others are mistreating me over and over, there could very well be an inner abusive pattern from many years ago playing out. Did I put it there? Probably not, but I might have attracted it, based on my VPZ. *The issue of how it got there is less relevant than knowing I can do something about it.* THIS—the Law of Reflection—allows me to see what I might otherwise miss.

How can I see how I am treating myself? What will allow me to see my real world? Sometimes we can't see anything at all except as a reflection. Understanding THIS has made such a difference!

Resetting my Vibrational Permission Zone

As I transform, so does my world. In that process, my VPZ automatically resets as well. It's all reciprocal and proportionate.

After all the years I've been practicing THIS, I can still trigger a VPZ alarm, but I've noticed the zone expanding as I learn to tolerate a more wonderful life. It's important to be gentle with ourselves in such a process. Some of us do best with a slow expansion toward a more wonderful life rather than sudden and big change.

We think we want it all now, but if we actually did receive it all in an instant, there are those of us who couldn't handle it. While that probably doesn't make sense to some people, if you've lived with a lot of orphans, you might understand what I'm describing. Slow and steady is best in these cases. We've all heard about people who went from poverty to great wealth through the lottery and ended up right back where they started, or worse. It's a powerful example.

Another caution: As my VPZ resets, everything transforms along with it. And as everything transforms, *orphans who refused to show up earlier now come out of hiding.* This is a good sign, although it took a while for me to understand that, because it doesn't always feel good.

Every so often I've felt like I'm right back in the war zone, zapped by a wounded aspect of myself—and one that isn't quite as easy on me as One was in the beginning. Now I see these as signs of progress. I might never be done dealing with these pieces in this lifetime—I mean Nirvana might be possible. I'm not there yet, but I'm on my way.

What to do if something old and ugly shows up? The Drench! Each and every time. I suggested earlier that I've had to get creative at times because these harder, deeper wounds are more closed off to love, but I come up with a new way every time. One activity I've added to my daily wake-up exercises is to sit under the waterfall in the Pool of Unconditional Love for a few minutes and to invite lingering orphans to join me.

I also like to say "The higher we climb, the deeper we fall" like the Josh Groban song, 'Let Me Fall'[33] suggests. Don't be alarmed if you experience a trip and fall occasionally. It's a sign of growth and expansion. I've had plenty of wonderful experiences that have shown me that I'm making progress—always keep your eyes open for those.

Certainly, Tom and I don't have the issues we used to have. OK. We're human; we still have challenges, but they are more like lessons that we want to learn that draw us closer together. There's rarely fighting, and I don't ever want to leave. THIS has been 100 percent effective—even better than Ivory soap.

Imagine a relationship in which there is no blame and where every disagreement is a basis for deepening love, a relationship that never grows old or boring. Imagine! Tom and I now have more thirty years together and almost a decade of relating based on THIS. As we face our aging bodies and sometimes flagging energy, Tom's hearing challenge, and my listening handicap, the one aspect that endures and prospers is our love.

*R*ight now, I am sitting in front of my marvelous curved computer screen, typing words that magically appear in front of me so I can read them. But I can only see them because they are external. They appear in my mind, but I have to type them into my computer in order to see them. Pretty incredible, right? Isn't that also a form of reflection? All ideas start inside—everything must originate there.

Does my marriage work the same way? Is my husband, who appears to be separate from me, a reflection of my inner world, a person I've attracted to show me myself? I believe so, which explains why I get so aggravated when he shows me something I don't want to see!

Aha! *So…those reactions I've had all these years are not reasons to leave my spouse—they are reasons to do my inner work?* Could be.

It is beyond my scope of knowledge to help someone who has suffered any form of long-term abuse, but there is help. When we become aware, we can act much more effectively to heal ourselves, but getting support is essential. If anyone reads this book and then says, "Oh, I'll just handle this myself," I'll be saddened.

Learning to love ourselves after being wounded is best achieved with the support of others—and *professional* others, I might add. I learned so much from my therapists. I worked on my problems over the course of years and applied myself to learning until I got to THIS.

Now, let's move on—no getting stuck here analyzing all the ways we've suffered. It's not necessary—awareness and release are key. Since the world outside of us shows us our inner world, we'll see any of this that pops up, if we're paying attention.

And guess what! Guess what! The good news is that I was able to resolve a lot of my inner trauma without blaming my husband or ever again leaving my marriage! What if that's possible for others? As I do my work, my external world changes because it has to. I've learned to do this skillfully enough that I spend much less time suffering. Just remember, I got help.

Finally, if any type of abuse is showing up regularly in your life right now, it is essential to recognize and deal with it. It may require you to remove yourself from a situation, particularly if actions against you are constantly violent or degrading. Please seek counseling or a shelter for yourself and, if necessary, your children. Nothing is gained by staying where one's life (physical, emotional, or otherwise) is in danger. The Women's Center in Waukesha, Wisconsin, saved me in so many ways!

But as we leave—and this is so important—we still benefit from practicing THIS, because if we don't, we can unintentionally attract more of the behavior we hope to be leaving behind. As anyone who has suffered abuse knows or eventually learns, *external abuse doesn't stop until we end it internally.* And THIS is an excellent way to do that.

Exhibit A

VIVIAN'S LIST OF SUBTLE ABUSES

The following list is for anyone who feels detached, blue, or stuck or can't help but see the world and its events as consistently negative. Perhaps one of these subtle forms of mistreatment has produced orphans who are begging for love and attention.

Vivian's List of Subtle Abuses:

1. <u>Abuse of Punishing</u>: Others foster an environment in which I was/am punished regularly and often, even if I had/have done nothing significantly wrong.
2. <u>Abuse of Rage</u>: Others take their anger out on me because they could not/cannot release it to the deserving party.
3. <u>Abuse of Disrespect/Bullying</u>: Others constantly tell me that I'm wrong, even pushing me around, making fun of me, hurting me because they can, or calling me names. Oh, and then they add that special cruelty of saying, "I was just kidding," or "I didn't mean to hurt you (again). Stop being so sensitive."

4. <u>Abuse of Indifference</u>: Others close to me are too busy for me. "Children should be seen and not heard." "Leave me alone; can't you see I'm busy?" I'm not sure where parenting with both hands texting on a cell phone comes in. It looks inattentive and denies children the privilege of eye contact.

5. <u>Abuse of Superiority</u>: Others regularly remind me that they are older, wiser, or more talented than me. (This is particularly aggravating if those people act as if I have no idea what they are talking about and feel like they have to explain things to me as if I were five years old.) We could all enjoy life much more if we treated one another as intelligent and asked questions before making assumptions. (Still a sore spot for me at my age!)

6. <u>Abuse of Rejecting/Disagreeing</u>: Others make it a habit to disagree with me, no matter what, and then combine it with number five.

7. <u>Abuse of Neglect</u>: Others responsible for my basic needs do not look after them. This affects children left to fend for themselves or placed in the care of abusive people.

8. <u>Abuse of Unprotection</u>: Others regularly allow me to be exposed to dangerous or harmful situations without any form of protection.

9. <u>Abuse of Overprotection</u>: Others are always with me, telling me what to do and how to do it; they are fearful that something could go wrong and don't allow me to have any time for my own exploration of the world around me.

10. <u>Abuse of Expected Performance</u>: Others regularly tell me what the expectations are and the consequences of not living up to them. (Such expectations are often unreasonable.)

11. <u>Abuse of Non-acceptance or Unforgiveness</u>: Others regularly make me feel responsible for things that go wrong and then refuse to forgive me. This is particularly harmful if I have done nothing wrong.

12. <u>Abuse of Self-Absorption (aka narcissism)</u>: Others expect me to always praise them and often negate me in the process. I only exist to make them feel good about themselves.

13. <u>Abuse of Religion (particularly as it diminishes women)</u>: Others regularly tell me that I am a woman and inferior to men; I am bad or sinful. They threaten me with hell so that I become fearful of a male God's ability to punish me eternally.

14. <u>Abuse of Positive Thinking</u>: Others regularly tell me that I need to be happy regardless of how I feel inside and don't allow me to cry or express angry feelings.

15. <u>Abuse of Language</u>: Others use derogatory words in conversation to make me feel bad about myself. This topic is being reserved for another book—it's too massive for *I Was a Yo-Yo Wife.*

16. <u>Abuse of Past Lives</u>: Sometimes there is no other explanation for a way we feel except that during a past life we were subjected to something that caused us to bring negative feelings about ourselves into this lifetime. Past-life regression therapy is amazing. I leave this discussion to the experts in that field.

17. <u>Abuse of Broken Promises</u>: Others regularly disappoint me by making promises and then not following through. Sometimes there's a good reason, but if I can't trust others to do anything but disappoint me, it's a form of abuse that settles in, especially in early childhood. It's even worse to go back on a promise or take it away as punishment when I had no idea that was a possibility.

Any one of these seventeen topics could be greatly expanded. My purpose here is to raise consciousness about them so that you can use THIS process to resolve their possible effects.

*T*his is the end of Part I. My goal has been to explain and share my discovery of the concept I call THIS. In the next part of our adventure, we explore the Seven Wonders of the Inner World that bring the benefit and beauty of THIS to light in my relationship with myself, my most intimate partner, and the Source of Life.

Part II

THE MAGNIFICENT SEVEN WONDERS OF THE INNER WORLD

Nine

Introducing the Magnificent Seven

The following are what I consider the Magnificent Seven Wonders of the Inner World. Let's go exploring and see if we find them in your Planet Me! If you missed them in the Clara Notes in the introduction, here they are again. I have divided them into the three categories as outlined in the Introduction although they are not able to be separated in life. Each of them influences the others:

Section A. The Wonders of My Relationship to Myself (Meology)
1. Everything I see around me is intended for me to be able to see what I believe about myself. I cannot help but create what lives inside me in my external world; the external and internal are inseparable.
2. I am creating my future right now. There is no blame; I am not a victim.
3. The most important goal for this lifetime is to deeply love and approve of myself, to know who that is, and to allow that profound sense of self to joyfully guide what I create.

Section B. The Wonders of My Relationship to My Most Intimate Partner

1. I am in exactly the relationship I need to be, for reasons I may have yet to discover. If I don't like what I find in my most intimate relationship, it's up to me to resolve what's causing my discomfort in my inner world.

2. Who I am in a relationship *with* is less important than *who I am being in that relationship.* I am either being my extraordinary true self or a hideously false imitation that my protective ego prefers.

3. I can leave a relationship as long as I recognize that I take my own issues with me; they will follow me wherever I go until I allow them to share their special wisdom.

Section C. The Wonder of My Relationship to the Source of Everything

I am deeply loved and connected to the Source of Everything that lives and breathes through me, whether I believe it or not. That Source is profoundly interested in me and cares about me to the *n*th degree.

If you thought Part I was interesting and mind altering, wait till you see what happens here in Part II. We will spend all our time in the inner world, the only place where everything is real and vital. While here, we will explore our relationship with ourselves, with our intimate partners, and Life.

To clarify, THIS taught me that we are each our own planet (or universe). So my Planet Me is different than your Planet Me. Whenever I use the phrase *Planet Me*, it's not only me referring to my Planet Me; you can consider your own Planet Me as well.

Before we take off, I'd like to prepare us for some concepts that might be objectionable at first and for any resistance that shows up.

First, expect resistance—it's a good sign.

Resistance to new discoveries is natural. It takes time to process and assimilate new ideas. We don't have to look very far to understand human nature in this regard. Simply observe what happens when someone suggests we do something differently than we have in the past. You might be someone who jumps up and down with joy and says, "Oh goody! I so wanted to change that anyway!" But many of us immediately want to retreat to our comfort zones with excuses and explanations that protect our little worlds. *Am I alone here? I don't think so.*

For instance, we might think it's very funny that anyone ever thought that the world was flat. But people were imprisoned and ridiculed, and some even died for believing it wasn't. Also, before we understood medical science and the germ theory, doctors didn't wash their hands before performing surgery, and thirdly, a common way to treat an illness was to remove blood from a person's body.

Check out the book *Infinitesimal: How a Dangerous Mathematical Theory Shaped the Modern World,* beautifully written by Amir Alexander. It describes how calculus, a mathematical necessity that has breathed life into modern technology was forestalled by the Catholic Church for over one hundred years and how without it, we would still live in the world of the mechanical industrial revolution without hope of deliverance.

Every generation has made its own discoveries on the backs of people who were considered heretics and lunatics. Taking a tour of your inner world may feel just that strange. It makes me wonder why we thrash so violently against the very theories that are meant to transform us. But we do.

So if anyone objects to visiting his or her inner world or thinks my Seven Wonders of the Inner World are strange, I absolutely understand. Feel free to disagree—even though these seven aspects are now proven to be some of the most basic laws of science and the universe. That's not meant to intimidate anyone; if you don't agree, you don't agree.

Imagine what a boring world it would be if we all agreed on everything! But locking in to an old world order because we're more comfortable there instead of venturing forth into what's possible isn't what we're here for.

*N*ext, a little anxiety and fear is normal.

It might be frightening to venture inside. Who knows what's lurking there? Just like new ideas often scare us, the concept of visiting your Planet Me can be daunting. Like in the Land of Oz, we might perceive that there's a frightening, boisterous wizard waiting to trap us in a foreign land (even if it is *inside*, so to speak). Anyone who has visited or lived in foreign countries knows how strange it feels; even moving to a new city can be terribly uncomfortable. (Tom and I just finished a one-month trip through South America, so we are very conscious of the various barriers that kept us from feeling like we fit in!)

But Planet Me is your very own inner world; you are its architect, its designer, and its most powerful citizen. Take a tour—if you'd like, come with me on a tour of Planet Me as I've discovered it to be and see what you think of the Seven Wonders I discovered. Remember to look for ways to have fun. It's your planet, and you can do what you want to!

The famous and beloved thirteenth-century Persian poet Rumi[34] is quoted as saying, "There is only one journey. It is inside." Modern science has shown this to be true. Let's not be afraid of what might show up. Let's be curious, because we have all the power to change anything we want to!

Section A

The Three Wonders of My Relationship to Myself

Ten

The First Wonder of the Inner World: 'WISIWIG', or *What I See Is What I Get*

*Everything I see in the world around me is intended
for me to be able to see what I believe about myself
on the inside of life; I cannot help but create that in
my external world. What I expect is what I see.*

—Vivian Probst

What you see is what you expect.

—Dr. Fred Alan Wolf[35]

There are those who say not to take what other people do or say personally—it's their issue, not mine. Yet to live fully in THIS, I accept that any person, place, thing, event, circumstance, and even the job I have or the person I married show up in my world only because I've given permission for it to be so. They are here by special consent for a divine purpose that is essential (notice the word *essence* here) to my highest well-being.

If I observe that my most intimate partner (or anyone else) is repeatedly cruel or unkind, I resolve it, not by blaming him or her and cutting myself off, but by recognizing that this person's attitude is an accurate reflection of my own inner need to be cruel or unkind to myself. As I resolve my own inner need to treat myself poorly, I banish all external factors. That's it! That's THIS in an acorn.

It's not my fault that I attract what I do; often it's because I can't see it until I see it playing out externally. It's my responsibility to become aware and to love myself out of this toxic pattern.

As I resolve my problems for myself by healing my inner traumas (orphans), my most intimate partner changes accordingly and in direct proportion to my degree of healing. In my case it meant that our marriage became indescribably wonderful and even now continues even now to amaze both of us.

Since the first five chapters have dealt extensively with this topic, let's move on.

Eleven

The Second Wonder of the Inner World: *What If This Is the Life I Ordered?*

I am creating my future right now. There
is no blame; I am not a victim.

- Vivian Probst

Many of us are continually frustrated (subconsciously)
due to the inner conflict of not really enjoying
the situation we've been driven to create.

—Karol Truman in *Feelings Buried Alive Never Die*[36]

No kidding. In *Death by Roses*, my main character, Mae Rose McElroy, discovers how wonderful life could have been *after* her life on earth is over. She would encourage all of us to get THIS while we're living. "But in all of it, Mae Rose saw that as she worked on what was going on inside of her more than what was going on in her marriage, the better her marriage became" (Probst 2015). Once we accept that we are creating all the time and that circumstances in our external lives are trying to get us to focus on the real world inside, everything changes.

When Mae Rose finally gained access to The Dial and was able to see how wonderful her marriage could have been, she was stunned. She was also more than a little miffed that she had to die to learn this, and then not even death could stop her in her determination to let Art know what she now understood. No, even though her Reflection Agent had clearly explained that initiating contact with earthly beings was absolutely forbidden and had consequences, she charged ahead with sometimes hilarious consequences.

The message of the Second Wonder of the Inner World was pretty powerful, and it stopped me dead in my tracks. According to Mae Rose, I couldn't fix my relationship with Tom if I didn't take advantage of the time I had left in this lifetime. *What kind of future did I want with Tom? Was I working at creating that, or was I sowing seeds of continued discord that would only lead to more misery?*

Waking up to the fact that I had a choice about the future of my relationship with Tom and that I was creating that future *right now* was the best gift I could have received. Learning that in our most conflicted moments, Tom was reflecting something inside of *me* imbued me with the determination to choose now what I wanted for the future. Once I understood that the challenges we had in our marriage were intended for my highest good and to help me heal my inner wounds, I was able to release any resentment against Tom. I think this stunned him.

It becomes intuitive. There's no conniving, no posturing, and no manipulating. I want a "knock-your-socks-off" relationship with my husband. I want what Art and Mae Rose missed out on. That's my focus now. I want it for myself as much as for Tom.

My friend, author Anne Wondra (2016), talks about being "healthy selfish" in *Relationship Rules of a Happy Woman*[37]—a book I highly recommend. I'm not being charitable and altruistic when I lay claim to the relationship I want with Tom. I'm being "healthy selfish," she says. I want that relationship with Tom for myself, probably more than I want it for Tom!

Taking care of the wounded orphans in my inner world is very healthy selfish. It opens the door to a life full of magic and miracles and gives me the freedom to create it. It's getting out of my own way so that all the possibilities I'd like to see can actually find their way to me.

When I learned through quantum physics that I am creating everything I see in the world around me—that it all originates inside first *before* it shows up outside, I got busy. Fun busy. I'm not a "catalog of the universe" woman as in "I want one of these and a bunch of those" (although those types of things show up all the time); I'm more of an inner-universe explorer, the careful art restorer who wants to discover the original painting of myself.

In other words, I have preferences—of course I do! —but I love to let Life surprise me by bringing into my world whatever is perfect for my life right now. I don't want a Santa Claus or a sugar daddy; I want a relationship. I choose to have a wonderful life; I act in that direction; I speak it, I dream it, and I embrace it—even, and especially, when it looks impossible. Then I shut up and allow it to show up. We have to accept that sometimes the results are not instantaneous in the external world, but they can be inside. Oh, to wake up and look forward to today, knowing that everything I can imagine for my life is creating itself right now!

Yes, those inner orphans still show up, particularly when I feel more success coming my way. I can still hear their voices booming, "You don't deserve that!" or "It will never happen."

I don't scream back. My orphans have taught me compassion for myself; that, in turn, allows me to show compassion for others. More than anything else, I want lots and lots of compassion in my world, especially from my husband, for the rest of our lives on earth. I want a soothing relationship, one that supports my expansion beyond the person I am today until the perfect portrait has been restored. This allows me to see how I'm doing with *that*.

When Mae Rose sees in her afterlife how she could have coped with the things she found most despicable about her husband (like his cigarette smoking), she wishes she'd been able to do that during their lifetime together. She does, indeed, return to earth, but it doesn't go the way she had intended (at all!). She teaches me that I can't really go back; the best moment to create the outcome I (healthily and selfishly) desire is *right now*.

*F*ocusing on what is wrong right now creates more of what is wrong in my future. I cannot help but create that to which I give my attention. And it is that to which I give my attention that I see coming to pass in my external world. By changing my focus from what I see as wrong externally to what I wish to become internally and treating myself as if what I want to become is already real inside of me, I have the highest probability for success.

Our natural tendencies are important to observe. If I tend toward negative future perceptions, it is possible that such a perception has been planted in my psyche by my parents or other vitally important people in my early years. It is as I become aware of this tendency that I can resolve it, but only if I am willing to do so. Therefore, it is paramount that I take any negative tendencies that exhibit themselves in the external world, particularly from my most intimate partner, as a reflection of my internal world. With this information, I can change my inner awareness, and what I see in my external world is transformed as well. If I am naturally optimistic and looking forward to wonderful discoveries, I am already on my path.

If you are anything like me, you have been raised to expect disappointment, pain, and suffering. I believe my mother even relished this part of life, as if she were following Jesus, who, indeed, suffered and was killed. The part that puzzles me now is why someone who believes that he or she has been saved by the blood of Jesus Christ would think that suffering is a good idea. I don't think that's the part of Jesus's life we're supposed to emulate.

I like to tell my evangelical friends to remember that *Jesus rose from the dead*; he went on to administer to his followers in an even more brilliant way. So my question became, *am I supposed to hang around the cross because Jesus died there, or am I to live the way that Jesus lived after he rose from the dead?* If I'm a Christian, I belong in the second group. I would hope every Christian feels that way, although my life experiences demonstrated how deeply focused they could be on sin, the cross, and the blood of Christ—none of which would merit any attention if it hadn't been for the resurrection. So I believe their focus is misplaced.

For the most part, I've not seen the point of staying at the cross. When people ask me if I believe in God, I say, "Absolutely! And I am part of that

Source of Life!" I come from that Source (whatever anyone calls it). I simply prefer to focus on living transformed. OK, I'm not saying I'm perfect, but I'd rather experience life based on that power rather than the pre-resurrection side. For those of you who are not of the Christian faith, I believe the same holds true. Live in love with the life that was exemplified in your Teacher. Choose suffering or love. (Psst—go with love).

I recognize that we've been hearing the phrase "What you think about, you bring about" for decades now, and it can be nauseating for someone to bring it up again. However, if, like me, you have a propensity to trip yourself up every time you take a step forward, there's a great opportunity here for growth and change.

What if I'm not sure I believe that's true? I don't have to believe something is true in order to take it for a test drive, do I? That's where I started in transforming my relationship with Tom. When I got the message that I was seeing almost everything incorrectly (I like the word *incorrectly* much better than *wrong*), I simply asked myself, *What if it's true? What if it's me who's causing what I'm seeing in my husband?* What if, indeed!

Twelve

The Third Wonder of the Inner World:
Meology, the Only Thing That Matters on Planet Me

This is the true joy in life, the being used for a purpose
recognized by yourself as a mighty one; the being a
force of nature instead of a feverish, selfish little clod
of ailments and grievances complaining that the
world will not devote itself to making you happy.

I am of the opinion that my life belongs to the
whole community, and as long as I live it is
my privilege to do for it whatever I can.

I want to be thoroughly used up when I die, for the harder I
work the more I live. I rejoice in life for its own sake. Life is
no "brief candle" for me. It is a sort of splendid torch which I
have got hold of for the moment, and I want to make it burn as
brightly as possible before handing it on to future generations.

—George Bernard Shaw[38]

*What good is it to the universe to have a planet filled
with souls who have no idea whatsoever why they
are here or what they are supposed to be doing?*

—CAROLYN MYSS, *SACRED CONTRACTS:
AWAKENING YOUR DIVINE POTENTIAL*[39]

Go ahead and get mad at me. Get it over with. Call me self-centered or worse. What right do I have to focus on *me?* Even if you now consider me to be a most narcissistic woman, please keep reading. If you stop now, you'll miss the most vital treasure of all. I call it Meology, the study of myself. It is the most important journey most of us never take. Long before we make a vow to love and cherish someone else "till death do us part," it is essential to make that promise to ourselves. I believe this is the reason so many marriages start off (and end) on the wrong track.

In *Death by Roses*, neither Art nor Mae Rose does any work on discovering who they are under the surface of life. Mae Rose never gets what she wants, and Art simply learns to live with his pain. But what if they had taken time to give themselves the opportunity to grow individually? Why don't we make this a priority in life?

George Bernard Shaw's quotation, from an essay titled "The Splendid Torch," which appears at the beginning of this chapter) speaks to the passion with which he lived his life.[40]

"Me, too!" I say. I don't want to face entry into the next life having left anything undone in this one. Mae Rose learns to take care of herself in her afterlife. Art learns to appreciate everything he couldn't stand about Mae Rose after it's too late to do anything about it. I don't want that to happen to me. What about you?

If you're reading this book, my guess is that we want the same things. What I have learned to love about Life is that it will never give up on allowing me to discover my inner world in its highest brilliance. The more willing I am to receive what my external world shows me and the more willing I am to be transformed into higher love and regard for myself, the more abundantly Life can reflect back to me the true nature of my highest self.

Oh my! Meology!

If I ruled the world, infants would be nurtured to love and respect themselves while they were still in the womb. Everyone would start studying Meology before he or she started school. And in school, there would be lessons and experiments and quizzes and evaluations meant to observe the core talents and passions that nurtured that unique and brilliant child's soul.

Teachers would be observers; each child would be embraced as having a specific drive and purpose, which would be permitted to develop in a loving environment, so that as his or her young life progressed, that child would have a deep appreciation for what it meant to be "me."

Oh, there's so much to know about ourselves—fascinating discoveries that not only transform our own experience of life but bring that influence to our outer world, as well! I believe that the person I really am (and that you are) is so very needed in this world—we're like a magical remedy for some of the world's worst woes. You might not think you're a big deal, but would you deny even a drop of the elixir of you to others if it would ease their suffering—especially if it doesn't require you to do anything but let your Life shine?

If you wonder, like I did, who you really are underneath the layers of opinions, warnings, preferences, and rules that others smeared over your original work of art, I'd like to share with you the self-study course I engaged in that taught me who I was. Yes, it's called Meology—the study of myself—and it took me on an I-opening (fun!) tour of my inner world. I consider it the most important course we **never** take in school. It's the complete study of who I am, and it can be absolutely thrilling. It certainly was for me!

Life completely personalizes our Meology tracks. Let mine serve as an example while *you* ask Life to prepare your own by bringing to your attention every specific detail that will polish the light of your particular brilliance. (Actually, I believe Life will attempt to do that, whether we ask for it or not; I found that allowing it to occur was pure fascination once I got out of the way.)

Opening the Door to Meology

Meology found me shortly after my divorce in 1980. It's important to say it that way because I wasn't looking for it as zealously as it was chasing me down. I was busy focusing on a new career and a new way of life. Life wanted me to know more.

Meology is different for every person. It has to take the lead, and it does as we allow it, once we open the door.

What door? A-dore. Get it? (*Don't you love it?*) If we never open it, if we don't allow ourselves to fall in love with who we really are (even when we're just beginning and have to sort of fake it), we can't attend the class. I must be willing to learn to love and admire myself as a creation of divine Love and light in the world; I must be willing to see myself differently and to begin to experience curiosity and wonder about who I am. It needs to captivate me in a healthy selfish way. Doesn't that sound wonderful?

Meology is not a course I expect to graduate from in this lifetime. I believe it occurs in stages as I become more and more open to seeing myself as I truly am. My guess is that some of us could not handle a sudden unveiling, but we can stand it if it's progressive. Remember the importance of patience.

True, learning THIS was years away yet, but beginning to change my perspective of myself opened me up to great wonders along the way. THIS simply added the key ingredient to Meology as I realized that my husband was reflecting my knowledge of myself. Meology gave me a window through which I viewed my inner world; THIS gave me a mirror.

I like using an analogy of self-discovery as an old, valuable painting that has been hidden. It's safe, but no one will ever see how amazing it is. What fun is that? Perhaps the image had to be painted over to be protected; perhaps others didn't see any value in the image and decided to cover it up with something they liked better. Are you with me?

Imagine that you're an incredible, valuable, and one-of-a-kind work of art, but life experiences and false, limited beliefs have hidden the original, so that no one—especially not YOU—could see who you really are underneath all the layers of other people's impressionistic images. You had to go into hiding until somehow even you forgot who you were. Imagine! No one could see your stunning masterpiece. Meology is the careful, loving restoration process every human being deserves.

That fake painting was my life story for decades, and I believe it is the experience many of us live. Even as I was growing up, I sensed that I was much different than the picture I saw. I ached to know myself without regard for what I was taught, but no one else would allow it, and I didn't know how to do it on my own. It was too frightening. Even when I could finally act on my own behalf, I was too conditioned to think poorly of myself to begin the process.

My life since I began studying my Meology has been the privilege of precisely and oh-so-carefully removing the fake cover-up without disturbing the beauty of what I had been terrified of seeing. It's like the best makeover ever. What's really cool is that we keep getting more and more beautiful! (Plus, I believe our inner beauty makes our outer beauty even more profound.)

The further and deeper I went into discovering my true essence, the more I had to decipher the difference between the real me and the version of me I had been for so long. Sometimes I couldn't tell who was who. That's why THIS was so important for me—it was a way to remove the false cover-up and get to my inner beauty through reflection.

With over six decades of life under my belt, I've noticed that as we get older, there are plenty of us who still say, "I'm not sure what I want to be when I grow up." We might intend it to be funny, but it's sad. I believe there is a deep sense of loss and regret if we haven't lived a life that expresses our originality. In fact, *the older I get, the more certain I am that this path of self-discovery is essential in order to get to the end of life with joy*. Oh, to know that I am being true to myself! To grow and expand with every passing day! It's never too late to take that step.

Meology got me started; THIS has helped me take it to a deeper level. Sometimes I can hardly wait to see what happens next. If life doesn't feel that way for you, let's get that engine started—today.

Oh my! Meology!

THE MYSTERY OF MY STORY

Can you see how the words *my story* and *mystery* are similar? I believe that each of us comes into the world and lives in a story that is an unveiling mystery— so often we can't see the bigger picture of what our lives on earth mean until later. Like Mae Rose until she received her Reflection, some of us tend to focus more on what "so and so" did to us that prevented us from having a wonderful life than on our role in creating the life we live.

In just the same way and for this reason, I believe in beginning with what *is*. That means telling the story of my (your) life as I (you) know it right now. In her book *The Vein of Gold*, Julia Cameron emphasizes this. She says, "By claiming our memories, we gain access to the creative energy they contain"[41] Most of us could use more creative energy—it holds the secret to who we are.

Our memories are like the black box on an airplane that tells us everything we need to know to fill in the blanks of our lives. Even the career-planning guide *What Color is Your Parachute?* by Richard Bolles[42] is based on his belief that "it's also about figuring out who you are as a person and what you want out of life." Oh yeah.

What follows is my story of Me. I am sharing a condensed version here as an example and to help you understand where I'm coming from, if that's important to you as you read this book. Use it as a framework if you'd like; just make sure you get yours written!

While I'm quite sure that your Mystory and mine are quite different, I want to share my experience—the absolute magic of digging for my soul. Life showed up with all kinds of self-discovery tools just when I needed them. It will do the same for you. What a ride!

Thirteen

In the Beginning: *Mystory* (*Writing the Story of Me*)

...the stories we choose to tell ourselves and cherish about ourselves are the true stories, the road map to the real, lantern-hearted self...We must deconstruct the negative story lines that hamper our growth.

- Julia Cameron[43]

Note: Some of this will be redundant because of what I have already shared in this book. However, if you're looking to write your own Mystory, you'll have an example here.

Now, let's take a quick break here and remember that your life makes a difference to the world. If you've never put your life story in a readable format because you think it's no big deal and who would really care anyway, you need to get going on this activity. Your life matters. My own story follows:

I came to life sooner than expected by about six weeks. This means I was underweight and spent several weeks of the beginning of my life in an incubator, removed from my mother's touch. (It was 1952; NICU today is a much different experience.) My parents like to share that I wore my father's hankies for diapers and that I was only as long as a dinner knife.

At the age of one year, I went into a coma from a high fever. The doctors told my parents that if I lived, I would not have meaningful brain function. Their pastor's communication with divine Love and light told a very different story. I lived, and for the most part, I'd say my brain function is just fine, thank you.

It's my opinion that this near-death experience caused other chemical and emotional alterations that made me even more sensitive and withdrawn than I had been at birth. I was afraid of everything, and having a troubled mother didn't help.

From the time I first understood the concept of death, I feared it. Saying my prayers that included "If I should die before I wake, I pray the Lord my soul to take" kept me awake and terrified. Having been blessed with an active imagination didn't help.

My father was in medical school when I was born. He and my mother shared a vision of serving God as missionaries after his medical training was complete. They were very poor; we lived in inadequate housing. Mom taught school to help pay the bills.

After bearing four children in fewer than six years, my parents' dreams were crushed when my mother (who was now working to help my father set up a medical practice) had a nervous breakdown shortly after my youngest sister was born. She was hospitalized, and we four were dispersed to various families until she recovered.

I know that my mother went through electroconvulsive therapy in the 1950s. I don't remember her before her treatment, but I lived with who she became afterward. I highly recommend the play Next to Normal, which describes one woman's post-ECT journey. When I saw it years later, it helped me to understand why I never felt connected to a mother's love and why she did not have love to share. It was so hard for me to watch; I wept in the ladies' room during intermission and just about didn't go back in for the second act.

Mom's condition took my parents off the life path they had envisioned. Dad set up a medical practice in a small Midwestern town; Mom tried to adjust to being a full-time mother and a doctor's wife rather than a missionary.

Being a conventional doctor's wife was not my mother's strong suit. As we grew up, we experienced her otherwise inexpressible rage at being so confined. I don't know when she began punishing us in inappropriate ways, but I remember enough of it to know that by any standards, she was abusive. We loved her and feared her.

I am of the firm opinion that when a woman is unable to express her true talents and divine gifts, she suffers, and that pain warps who she becomes. When Mom blamed herself for being the reason she and her husband could not fulfill what they perceived as the purpose in their lives, I believe she became enraged at herself and took it out on others, which is why she punished her children so frequently.

It became important for me to hide in order to protect myself. I was already the introvert of the family. That and my mother's unpredictable behavior compounded my preference for reading, writing, and being alone as I grew up. I had a few friends but felt terribly awkward and shy around people, especially adults. My other siblings were far more social than me, which isolated me further. Being the local doctor's daughter put me in the limelight more than I could bear. So I hid.

But oh! I loved to learn new things! My older sister taught me to read before I started school, so I was always ahead of the class. I was also smart enough that I'd get picked on for it. All I wanted was to be like everyone else. That would never happen.

We converted from the Baptist-flavored denomination we were being raised in (I don't recall any church from my early life) to Lutheranism when I was six years old. Years later my father explained that he was angry at God for my mother's illness, which had taken them away from their vision for their lives. But I liked the church, and I the parochial school we attended.

I wasn't pretty—anyone will tell you that. My older sister was the beauty; I was more like the ugly stepsister. My eyes were crossed, so I had to have two eye surgeries and wore glasses from the age of three. What an expensive child

I was for my parents, and I'm so grateful that they took care of my physical need.

At about nine years of age, I got so frustrated with how the Bible was written that I decided to rewrite it. I crashed in the Genesis genealogies, a bit irritated that Eve was considered the sinful one and that family lines were followed through men. It's just that I was always rooting for the female gender, since we were such underdogs. It would become much more than that as I grew older. My commitment to finding equality for women became a torch I still carry.

As I tell my husband, I'm not a feminist—I'm an "equalist." (When women share equally in government positions, when women and men earn equal pay, and when we care as much about women's health as we do our male counterparts, I'll be more satisfied. And no, I'm not running for office any time soon.)

Just before I turned thirteen, my parents recommitted themselves to the God of their youth and pledged themselves once again to mission work. This I remember although I had no idea what it would mean to my life. This time, they found a missionary society that would accept them, in spite of my mother's past problems.

We left the Lutheran Church and were suddenly at the deepest level of the evangelical world imaginable. It was akin to taking a vow of poverty and casting off the material world. We sold our luxurious home and almost all our belongings to move into a tiny apartment in the mission's training center. Mom and Dad slept in the living room; my two sisters and I had to share a room for the first time; my brother slept in a closet.

This move was my first introduction to public school; it was also the beginning of being seen as "one of those religious freaks." I had few friends, except for the other MKs (missionary kids) at the mission, who were always pushing the 'thou shalt not' religious envelope we lived under. More than once, I had to leave a group event because I didn't want to do the things all the other kids had in mind. I wasn't one of them, and I knew it—no matter how hard I tried, I didn't fit in either world.

We moved every year during the time my parents were in training. It was good for me to expand my introverted horizons to include others; but it was impossible to settle into a way of life that suited me, and the taunting and abuse from other kids, especially on the school bus, was awful. I wasn't getting any prettier either, and my posture was hideous (a sure sign of childhood abuse, I would learn much later).

In my freshman year of high school, throngs of boys would line the hallway to the classroom and heckle any girl that wanted to get to class on time. A student in my English class would follow me out of the classroom and kick my heels until they bled each day (and ruined my stockings). I said nothing about this to anyone, including my parents. But I suffered—I thought it was what Jesus would want me to do.

That same year I had an English teacher who told me I had writing talent. I will never forget her. My parents enrolled me in a Christian correspondence writing course because they sensed my desire; I could better cope with life around me when I had a pen and paper in hand.

It was also the year that my mother's inability to conform to being an appropriately submissive woman caused her to be publicly humiliated in front of the other missionaries in training. They were not permitted to speak to her until she repented.

You see, although my mother had been raised to be a good Christian woman, (and we had seen plenty of documents to prove that), the woman I lived with had a feistiness that could bring out the worst in others. She was strong and bossy, very much like her mother, her mother's mother and so on.

During our missionary training days, I remember how mom would see other students behaving badly—particularly the men. She would take it upon herself to help them change their ways by pointing out their errors. I think she even kept a book about these events. This activity called 'personal ministry' was encouraged by the mission. Students were supposed to call each other out when they felt someone was being unchristian.

Mom was very, very good at this. She was bold and insightful. And yes, she could be mean.

When I got home from school on the day that her humiliation happened, my mother was weeping on her bed. It was the day her spirit broke, and I decided to leave home.

With complete sincerity, I had wanted to visit a missionary school. While this was extremely unconventional, my parents were able to transact permission for me to spend my sophomore year in high school at one of the mission's schools. It was on the Amazon River just outside of Manaus, Brazil. My parents were close friends with a couple there who agreed to sponsor me. It was a fabulous experience; I benefited from being on my own, even though the kids at school teased me about how "intellectual" I was. I was even elected to student council.

It was the relief I needed from my mother's resurgent trauma. My dorm parents were angels; I swam and bathed in the Amazon (as long as I wasn't bleeding, since piranhas are attracted by blood). I visited leper colonies and slept in wide hammocks when I was visiting other kids from school during holiday breaks. I became deeply committed to God's work.

By the time I came home, my parents had moved to another mission-training location, where my father was able to build a medical center and treat missionaries who were home on furlough. We were happy there; it was my junior year of high school; the kids were kind. Mom ran the medical center's office.

For my senior year of high school, we moved to a rural community in Ontario, Canada, so that my father could begin teaching missionary students at another of the mission's training facilities. That's where I met Alvin, the man I would eventually marry. Public school became a nightmare again. This time I was a "Jesus freak" and a "Yankee." My panic attacks began.

When it was time for me to decide about my future, I knew what I wanted to do—go to college and become a writer. My parents supported this idea, but I was too timid and too deeply set in the ideology I had been taught by that time.

I had spent years hearing about how important missionary work was; I didn't feel right about pursuing something I wanted that wouldn't do anything to save people from hell. So I gave up my dreams and began training for missionary work.

While I was in Bible school, Alvin expressed interest in me, and we dated, first by letters, then through our year and a half of Bible-school training. He was not the first boyfriend I ever had—he was the second. My parents had not approved of my first boyfriend due to religious differences. I can still remember my broken heart when we parted.

I know Alvin loved me—I didn't know anything about the feelings one should have for another person. I assumed I was in love with him, and when he asked me to marry him, I said yes. I liked him; my mother didn't. She was quite opinionated about me needing a stronger man—which Alvin wasn't. I had no idea what she meant. In the mission, lots of young people were falling in love, marrying, and going to the mission field. I assumed Alvin and I would do the same.

Our marriage was not easy for either of us. We were very poor. Alvin's work was more important than mine. He was social, and I was not. I didn't know how to cook—I tried, but he lost twenty pounds in our first year together.

While I tried to be a submissive wife, I simply didn't agree with him on so many levels that I continually had to fight my urge to tell him off. I noticed that plenty of women in the mission felt the same way about their husbands, so it didn't alarm me. The blame pattern was already firmly instilled in my life, so I assumed that was just the way marriage was. I wasn't necessarily happy, but that really didn't matter—what mattered was that I was being obedient to God.

Alvin and I had two children born to us while we were in training, a wonderful girl and boy. When we left for our first five-year mission trip to Senegal, West Africa, in 1978, Hannah and Lincoln were four and two years old. I remember saying good-bye to my family, enduring the long plane flight, and being met at the mission guesthouse, where I felt welcomed and curious about our new lives.

However, once we left there to move to the mission school while the mission decided where to place us on a more permanent basis, I suffered. The heat was unbearable for me—I couldn't sleep. We had been trained to live under difficult conditions, but caring for my children and husband when they all came down with a tropical illness was beyond my capacity. Everything felt wrong. The blinders came off, and for the first time, I had to face the reality of the life I had chosen. It became clear that I didn't belong in the life I was in, and I couldn't share my heart with Alvin without feeling wretchedly sinful. Women's opinions didn't count for much, and it would break his heart if he knew.

Without a telephone line to call home, surrounded by curious African villagers, having very little money, trying to cook meals and live without running water, dealing with worms that bore their way into my children's bellies, and working so hard to be a good Christian wife, my spirit of dedication melted in the African sun. I so wanted to do God's will; I just couldn't figure out what that was any longer. Everything I had believed was up for grabs.

I began to question everything: Why was God a man and not a woman? Were men really better or closer to God than women? Why, if God created us in his (?) likeness, were we considered miserable sinners who had to be saved? These African people had a different culture and belief system than we did— did that make it wrong? Were they really on their way to hell? Was there a hell?

I didn't like the part of the predominantly Muslim culture that required wives to walk behind their husbands or allowed men to have any number of wives they could afford. But I would watch the African women carrying their baskets of food and laundry on their heads as they headed here and there. I listened to them talking, laughing, and singing, and I was jealous! They didn't appear to have as much of a problem with it as I did. And who was I to talk? I didn't have to walk behind my husband in a physical sense but in so many other ways, it didn't feel much different.

*O*ne night our mission team was invited to observe a tribal-dance ritual from a distance. As I heard drums beating and people singing and being a community (even though I had been taught that they were worshiping a false god), all I wanted to do was run and join them!

Night after night, under a mosquito net, as the mud-brick house we lived in released the heat of the day, I wrestled with what to do. It took only a few months for me to break down. I had to tell the truth—not only to my husband, however. It was a confession to an entire committee of men who ran our mission operations. I was rebuked, anointed with oil, and prayed for, so that I would return from my sinful ways. It got so bad that I asked God to take my life—not just because of my level of despair, but, God forgive me, because it would be the easiest way out.

I had no source of income to support me; if I left my marriage, I would be excommunicated and thrown into a world I had never been a part of. Whatever structural framework there was to my short twenty-eight years of life would implode, which is exactly what happened.

We returned from Africa only six months after we had arrived, and it was completely my fault. We were excommunicated; our divorce was finalized in 1980 after I surrendered custody of our children to my husband, who truly believed he was the better parent because he maintained the faith. I lost almost everything familiar to me. My parents wrestled with what I had done; we did not speak much for the next three years. My brother was in Africa, which made communication difficult; my sisters were supportive—at least they talked to me.

My journey into my own Meology began when I collapsed on the doorstep of The Women's Center in Waukesha, Wisconsin, ill in body, mind, and soul. Without their support, I don't know what would have become of me. They nurtured me in every way and, very practically, showed me how to find a job and help support my children—I call it being born again. I recall the day I received a job offer—I was so terrified that I told the company that I would consider it and get back to them. Then I went to bed and called The Women's Center. After a brief discussion, I had the courage to call back and accept the job. That's how much The Women's Center made a difference in my life.

Bouncing from the excruciating pain of being divorced from my children and my family to the unbelievable exhilaration of freedom from religious restraint, I began a career path in real estate property management and enrolled in night school to start to earn a real college degree. I inhaled self-help books in order to get to know who I really was. It might be a trite phrase that makes you want to gag, but if, like me, you've spent decades ignoring the passionate desires that live inside you, it is a celebration of coming home.

My Meology course had begun, and it would begin to remove layers of false beliefs so that I could change the course of my life as I began to know the real person behind the mask of a false identity and to learn that I was much more than a miserable sinner. Learning that what I thought and what I wanted to explore in this lifetime was vitally important and not wrong to pursue set me free. Hello, life! I studied whatever I could get my hands on. I read Leo Buscaglia's books as if they were dark-chocolate candy[44]; I took the Myers-Briggs Personality Type Indicator and was stunned at how accurately it defined me[45], which meant it was OK to be who I was— an introvert with marvelous gifts. Can you imagine the freedom of knowing that my shyness and lack of desire to be ultra-social were gifts of my personality? I read *What Color is Your Parachute?*[46] I did all the exercises.

Finding *Creative Visualization* by Shakti Gawain[47] in a small bookstore in downtown Chicago, where I was taking courses to expand my career path, began what has become a lifelong journey of visualizing and affirming what I desire in my life. (I believe it attracted Tom to me as well.) Believe it or not, a business client taught me my numerology based on my maiden name and date of birth. It was magical!

It was inevitable that I would get around to astrology, which my religion had taught me was from the devil. It wasn't; it isn't. It's marvelous and so accurate. From there I learned about the energy of stones from my new friend Anne; she also introduced me to angel and oracle cards, which I continue to study every Sunday morning.

Everything was so new, so wonderful! The world I had not known was opening up to show me my wonder. Everything I was learning I would share with my children on the weekends they were with me. I wanted them to have the opportunity to think for themselves even while they were young.

I was so transformed that people who had known me before didn't recognize me. Eventually the rift between my parents and me mended, although I no longer shared their religious views.

As I traveled around the country doing tax-consulting work for the affordable-housing industry, I "happened" across two books that would change the trajectory of my life even more significantly. First came Leadership and the New Science by Margaret Wheatley[48] and then a book co-written by her and Myron Kellner-Rogers of a book titled A Simpler Way[49]. I felt the rush of a refreshing breeze come into my life, and I became an avid student of quantum science, even though I could hardly believe what I was reading.

In 1990, Life conspired to bring me the opportunity to have my own consulting business, a concept I had never considered, although I am the first to confess that I could look at a real-estate business, tell you why it wasn't working and what to do about it. However, I hadn't intended to have a business of my own. Tom was supportive, and my consulting business was launched. I can see now that Life needed me to be free of the constraints of being an employee (not that being an employer is any less time consuming or demanding), but it did give me control of my own schedule, which would shortly become very important.

My panic attacks returned shortly after this. Oh la la! Nothing like it! By that time, I was usually traveling alone across the country to conduct training events. I loved all of it but was worried about the toll being taken on my health by the stress of my marital problems and the work of keeping my business running.

From the first time I woke up unable to breathe and sure I was dying, I was terrified. That's when my marital issues cracked wide open. Tom simply could not relate to me as a weak and frightened woman, such as I became at those times. He wouldn't have anything to do with me except to scold me. It was infuriating and frightening.

I remember one time when I was at an airport on an emergency flight home because my heart rhythm wouldn't settle and my blood pressure was erratic. (This was later diagnosed as the circadian-rhythm dysfunction mentioned in Chapter 13. Once diagnosed, I had to stop my travel for months while medication enabled my body to recalibrate itself.)

As I waited anxiously for the next flight home from Logan International Airport, a medical attendant checked me over and stayed with me until it was time to board the plane. During our conversation, she asked how my marriage was. I was shocked until she shared with me that she had once had similar symptoms-- that after she left her marriage, they went away.

Perhaps she was right, but it wasn't the solution I was seeking. Even though I had left Tom often-- even though I yo-yoed-- something kept bringing me back. Once I learned THIS, I knew why Life had kept me in my marriage. If I had left Tom, I would have carried all my issues with me. I would have gained nothing.

Even though I felt distanced from Tom—when I felt he was unloving to me after my emergency and I didn't know how to bear it—I will always be glad I stayed

I'm not suggesting staying as an act of putting up with or suffering through a 'you made your bed so you have to lie in it' kind of attitude. Not at all. I stayed for what I needed to learn because somehow I must have understood that leaving wasn't going to solve the problem, and that I was in some way contributing to the issues we had. That's what I wanted to understand and fix—just my part.

It can be hard to admit the role we have in the drama that plays out with a spouse. I had a lot to learn. I suppose Tom did, too, but I can't say what that was for him. I can only share my story. I stayed; I continued my inner work. Much, much later I would be able to see how my own insensitivity to Tom's diagnosis of prostate cancer years earlier had come home to roost. If Tom was intolerant of my condition, so had I been about his. Our marriage had been difficult and his cancer, for me, felt like another strike against us. How could I have forgotten how I treated him?

The next big event in my life occurred when rather suddenly, my children returned to me—a marvel I could not have anticipated. They were old enough now to make their own decisions about where they wanted to live. It came up while I was traveling—I remember exactly where I was—in Saint Louis on business and also visiting my family. We were shopping for dinner ideas at a grocery store, when Tom called me to tell me that Hannah and Lincoln wanted to come to live with us. They were feeling urgent about it and their father supported the idea. Of course Tom and I said yes. I could hardly believe that Life would be so kind to bring them back to me for the few remaining years of their time in high school.

I'd like to say that we all lived happily ever after, but there were significant adjustments for all of us. Love pulled us through. The day my youngest child, Lincoln, moved out of our home into his own apartment and I realized that I was no longer an active mother, I went into a depression for about six months. It was as if I had just been getting used to having my children in my life again when they had the audacity to grow up and leave home. And then they married and bore children. Grandchildren! Precious, adorable, intelligent grandchildren. Such unconditional love came from them. Five marriages for our five children and a growing brood of grandchildren. We needed a larger home.

In 2007, Tom and I moved into a new home, built and customized to our specifications as the house of our dreams. (If you haven't built a house with your spouse, you might want to know that it is one of the most noted causes for divorce in America.) Still, we survived, although I completely lost my sanity when the kitchen counters were delivered, and they were pink!

In our new environment, which was gorgeous beyond my wildest dreams, a savage sense of unworthiness attacked. I didn't deserve to have such a beautiful home! And the money I was earning? It was too much. I still hadn't learned that when I crossed over my VPZ, I couldn't be happy with any of it, no matter how hard I tried. Furthermore, I had to find a way to punish myself. That's how my VPZ worked. If I stepped beyond its boundaries, I had to pay.

My inner world was in turmoil. I lived with the voice that said, "Who do you think you are, living in such a wonderful place? How dare you!" As Truman says in Feelings Buried Alive Never Die [50]) (which I would not read until 2016), the feelings I had carried throughout my life had not died. "Those feelings," she says, "are not dead unless they are resolved." Mine weren't, and they came out of the woodwork to accelerate their campaign to keep me from feeling any joy and wonder.

It was truly ugly; I felt out of place and simply couldn't enjoy our new home. Once again my yo-yo came out as the pressure built, and in my customary fashion, I held Tom responsible. I left again; this time the pain was so great that I packed more of my things. I was sure my marriage was over. But once again, after taking time to soothe myself (usually in a hotel room for a day or two or while I was traveling for business, except for that three-month sabbatical we had taken years earlier), I came back. And then March 26, 2008 arrived—the day my sister died.

*L*earning THIS was wonderful; writing *Death by Roses* took THIS and anchored it into my life so I would know how to live a wonderful life in this lifetime. When I finally got around to taking the story to heart, I was stunned by how much it applied to Tom and me—how my perceptions of our relationship had been based on my own critical self-judgments that were usually erroneous. My need to blame him for my suffering was an old habit that needed to be taken out and shot.

With sass and humor, *Death by Roses* taught me that it was better to see my husband from a loving perspective rather than to wait and find out *after this life was over* that we could have had a wonderful life together. (Imagine that!) I so wanted that *right now*. I'll always be glad that Life stopped me in the hallway and taught me THIS and then gave me the story to write. I got it. To leave this marriage was to leave the opportunity for a wonderful life!

Life knows what will work best for each of us. I will always be glad that Life used my love of writing fiction to get my attention through a romantic comedy. I mean, if you have a lesson to learn, wouldn't it be fabulous to get it while laughing your ass off? That's what *Death by Roses* did for me.

Fourteen

Your Meology: *The Coronation of You!*

*Each of you is made, designed, with a uniqueness, one of a kind.
This uniqueness is the key to your purpose. Have the courage
to be yourself. Have the courage to speak your mind. Have the
courage to follow your heart and your purpose will be fulfilled.*

—Beth Christiansen in *Daily Meditations: 100 Days
of Love and Light for Your Spiritual Growth*[51]

As I stared at the full moon through the window of my writing study, I could see its Mona Lisa smile. "Just how are you going to squeeze this profound topic into a chapter of your book?" it seemed to ask. That's when I knew that someone else would be writing it from a more authoritative standpoint than I ever could.

Here's the thing. I've told you what I studied that helped me to deeply understand the person I was—my greatness. It wasn't hard; are you kidding? It was *fascinating*. And essential. Oh, if only we were all required to study ourselves in school! If we could all sit down together (or even if a husband and wife could do it with each other—or we could do it with our children), how wonderful! If only we would take the time to discover that original painting that lies under the gobbledygook!

Dealing with any trauma plastered over the essence of ourselves is an essential key to getting to the real person each of us is. Dr. David Richo[52] (2008) says, "Once we say yes without stammer or stutter to how the past played out for us and truly let go of it, we make room for adult issues, such as building self-esteem, successful relationships, and spiritual consciousness." So true! For many of us, unpacking suitcases of old memories is part of the housecleaning necessary to the process of living a full adult life, and let's be honest—some of us might not be hoarders in the reality-show sense, but if others could see our inner worlds, we would be convicted.

During my research I learned how critical (interesting word—*critic-al*) it was to know and love the person I truly am. If I don't delight and amaze myself, it's 100 percent possible that lack of self-worth is holding me back, confirming that what I've (erroneously) been led to believe about me is true.

How could anything be more important than rediscovering our wonder—our greatness—than coming to adore the person we are? We are not here to mimic others or to be good little boys and girls for the rest of our lives, according to someone else's definition. How utterly boring and disheartening! We are here to be our wonderful selves, to cherish who that is, and to be that openly.

THIS process allows our individual Meology to sparkle in a glorious way because we are able to remove reflections that do not empower us (sort of like taking off a lipstick color we don't like). Please note: there are no shortcuts out of Meology. There's no cheating or having someone else do all the homework. Did I just hear you say, "Shucks?"

Meology isn't a product for sale, but it is an incredibly amazing adventure if you're up for it. The first thing to get over is the sense that you are not important enough for this work; the cover-up, of course, is that there is no time. Yes, I know, there really isn't, except that it really takes no time at all, and if we can just allow the idea to exist—if we can just give it permission to be possible—it will take us on a rocket ride to who we really are. It took years for me to get to that permission point, but I'm so glad that I'm stubborn and relentless. And would anyone really mind studying herself or himself for the rest of that person's life? Growing more deeply in love with who he or she is and sharing that wonder with the world? I mean, really—would that bother anyone?

I hope you consider yourself important enough to study yourself! If you haven't already done so, remember to take that important vow to yourself. *Every one of us should have a time in our lives when we make these commitments to <u>our own selves</u>! How can we make these promises to others unless we know our own selves well? We must learn to do this for ourselves. We must!*

Taking this vow is one of the first steps. We could make it a ceremony! If you can't take time for that in your life right now, you can still honor your commitment to yourself. I would suggest creating a sacred space and gathering a few of your favorite, special treasures. I would light a candle or use one of those great nonflammable imitations. Try to find a quiet, private space, even if it's just for a few moments. Oh, and a journal to record the date would be marvelous. Then take three deep breaths, and repeat the vow below or make up your own. If I had my way, every person would learn and take this vow before committing to a relationship with another person. That's how important I feel this is! Now, imagine standing in front of a group of family and friends (or a mirror—see Louise Hay's book *Mirror Work*), and repeating the vow below to yourself.

A sample vow to myself:

"I (insert your name), promise to love, honor, and obey the truest sense of myself and to live in the most glorious sense of who I am that I can imagine. I promise to respect, nurture, and live in a way that allows my innermost gifts to be shared with the world, and I promise to do this forever without shame."

Oh la la! I can hear the cathedral bells chiming in celebration!

f we don't make ourselves a priority—and because we don't—we become lost to the wonder of who we are and the incredible gifts we bring to the world.

Here's the catch, particularly if we're in an intimate relationship and it's not working that way we wanted it to: it's very hard to make promises to others for the rest of our lives if we don't even know ourselves! It is, as I said earlier, why I believe so many relationships fail. How can we marry well if we don't know ourselves? I believe that women, in particular, *spend so much time trying to be what we think others want us to be.* If only we used all that time to learn who we are so that we attract partners who reflect our love and appreciation for ourselves back to us!

You're fascinating! Oh, I know you might not necessarily agree…I know you don't think you have time to explore your inner world. (Humbug.) Yes, I heard that comment—yes, I understand. But in my dreams, I see it—can you imagine a course of study all about YOU learning about yourself—and when you finish the course, we all attend to celebrate?

There's a coronation, trumpets, a crown, a gown, or tuxedo, if you'd like—the whole works—as you are declared king or queen of your own life! Of course you can have all the trimmings—why, you can even change your name if you want to! Some people are even changing their gender in order to feel more authentic.

How about a new piece of jewelry that you promise yourself you will wear every day in honor of the occasion of remembering who you are? The ideas roll around in my head—I hope they stimulate you to action.

If you decide to take yourself on this journey, Julia Cameron's books are a good investment. She makes self-discovery fun, and she keeps you on track by giving weekly assignments. Her book *The Artist's Way*[53] jumped off a bookshelf into my arms many years ago. Watch what comes across your path once you decide that your Meology is important. As mentioned earlier, the bibliography of this book could also be helpful.

On several occasions throughout this book, I've mentioned the importance of supportive professionals who assist us on our journey. I've had several, but none more long term or deeply committed to helping me than Dr. Boris Matthews, a Jungian psychologist and wise counselor.[54] We go back many years, and I can think of no one better able to lay out some principles on how to take your own journey to personal greatness than this man who has been so integral to mine.

You see, I do not have credentials to advise anyone on such extraordinarily essential matters as discovering your preferences, your talents, and your own life purpose, but Boris does. I asked him to write the following section. The following are his words and ideas from many years of experience with many, many clients. (It is my opinion that this type of analytical psychology well serves those interested in studying their own Meology.)

"How to Know Who You Are" by Boris Matthews, PhD

He writes, "The most effective invitation to launch your Meology journey is meaningless suffering.

When you no longer know why you are living as you are living—the time has come for you to undertake serious self-discovery.

When you repeatedly notice that you betray your truth—that's an invitation to take the first step.

When you notice—again—that somebody else's notion of who you are has more power over you than your sense of who you are—that's an invitation to take the first step.

When you say yes but are too afraid to say no—that's an invitation.

When you can't say yes but are unsure of your no—that's an invitation. Any invitation to take the first step on your Meology journey is good enough.

All these—and all the other first steps—boil down to this: You begin to recognize the voice that says, "Something's not right. Something doesn't feel right. Something doesn't suit me. It's so vague. It must be that I'm imagining it."

You're not imagining it.

If you wait long enough, your suffering will get worse, and the call to self-knowledge will become louder.

A dear friend puts it very simply: "Know yourself. Be yourself. Tell others yourself. Forget yourself. Be." When you can work the first three steps, the fourth and fifth steps are a breeze. We'll begin with step number one: Know yourself.

Knowing oneself can be a lifelong adventure, but it often begins in fear and trembling, which scares off some people. Getting to know oneself can be scary because you are discovering that other people's views of you—their sense of who you really are—fits you like somebody else's shoe, and although walking in that shoe may be very familiar and you know how to do it without limping, it really doesn't feel right.

Begin by paying attention to yourself and keeping track of what you notice. Notice when you feel in sync with what's going on. Notice when you feel less than fully in sync with what's going on. Like I said, don't kid yourself. You don't have to be miserable and suffering the torments of the damned to be registering some important information. Subtle is good.

This "noticing" that you're practicing is the initial step in getting to know more of what and who you are. You will make use of this "noticing" for the rest of your life. It will serve you well: from making fine adjustments to creating major overhauls. Here's what you are doing as you notice: you are getting to know, firsthand and personal, what you really are, what really suits or doesn't suit you, what appeals to you, and what repels you. As I like to say, you are calibrating the instrument of life: you.

Vivian's story is exemplary. Recall what Vivian writes about her mother:

> I am of the firm opinion that when a woman is unable to express her true talents and divine gifts, she suffers, and that pain warps who she becomes. When Mom blamed herself for being the reason she and her husband could not fulfill their perceived lives' purposes, I believe she become enraged at herself and took it out on others, which is why she punished her children so frequently.

"True talents and divine gifts" come as our birthright. We don't earn them. We're born with true talents and divine gifts. Vivian's mother embraced an image, a belief, of her life purpose. That might be the right life purpose for some people, but it poisoned Vivian's mother with rage; she became enraged at herself and took it out on others.

In *The Marriage of Heaven and Hell*, William Blake wrote a painfully insightful line: "He who desires but acts not, breeds pestilence."[55] Not knowing one's desire breeds pestilence. Vivian's mother could not honor her desire, if she even recognized it, and Vivian's story of her childhood and early adult life tells the pestilence bred of her mother's attempt to live a life that didn't suit her, a life that really wasn't in her to live. Vivian's mother was born to live a different life: her very own life.

The life we are intended to live exists as a "seed" in us. Our task in life is to recognize that "seed" and cultivate it into the full flower of authentic Self.

Vivian has always had a strong instinct for authenticity of Self. "At about nine years of age, I got so frustrated with how the Bible was written that I decided to rewrite it." Not bad for a nine-year-old. Vivian was still connected to her authentic core, to what Jungians call the Self.

In her experience of missionary school and mission work, Vivian sensed something important. Although refracted through fundamentalist theology and doctrine, there was something "real" behind the words. Yet in spite of the support from her high school English teacher and her parents, who enrolled her in a Christian correspondence writing course, she "didn't feel right" about pursuing something she wanted "that wouldn't do anything to save people from hell." Indoctrination overrode her connection to Self.

In her marriage to Alvin, her first husband, Vivian continued to suffer the conflict between what church doctrine prescribed—trying to be a submissive wife—and a clear recognition: "I simply didn't agree with him on so many levels that I continually had to fight my urge to tell him off. I noticed that plenty of women in the mission felt the same way about their husbands, so it didn't alarm me."

What a heartbreaking admission: "So it didn't alarm me."

When we hit bottom, the only way left is up:

Without a telephone line to call home, surrounded by curious African villagers, having very little money, trying to cook meals and live without running water, dealing with worms that bore their way into my children's bellies, and working so hard to be a good Christian wife, my spirit of dedication melted in the African sun. I so wanted to do God's will; I just couldn't figure out what that was any longer. Everything I had believed was up for grabs. I began to question everything.

She "began to question everything" and "ached to know" herself, and *that* conflicted with what she had been taught. The conflict between conditioning—what one has been taught—and being too frightened to act on one's own behalf nags our attention. Whatever Made Us—God or the universe or nature—protests what other people have made us into. Human beings are not blank slates or empty computer disks that somebody can program at will. Vivian's aching to know herself, in conflict with what she had been taught, *revealed* that her family and church environment violated her in fundamental ways.

The mind encodes everything we experience in "clusters" called complexes, held together by a specific emotional tone or "flavor." As C. G. Jung reminded a university audience in 1934, "Everyone knows nowadays that people 'have complexes.' What is not so well known, though far more important…is that complexes can *have us.*"

Complexes are a normal feature of the psyche. They can range from painful and troubling to pleasant and uplifting. A souvenir purchased on a delightful vacation can activate our complex of memories and experiences of the places, people, adventures, and surprises we encountered. Likewise, we have less pleasant complexes: mental and bodily memories of hurts we have suffered, infused with the emotional pain we felt and still do experience when something reminds us of the original—or the chronic—noxious experience.

Psychological/spiritual wounds and conditioning develop as clusters of experience held together by emotion, that is, complexes. In the case of conditioning, the emotion often has the quality of "should": "I *should* do this or that." "I *should* be a good Christian wife," was what Vivian felt at the time. For several years Vivian had lived in a family and community atmosphere that emphasized submission, belief, and service. In Africa, something in her rose up in protest to her life experience and learning of the previous several years. The emotion that bound together her identity complex made up of her sense of herself, of her family and community, and what it was to be a "good Christian wife" had a "should" quality. And she couldn't carry on with business as usual.

Activated complexes have energy. Similarly, a powerfully moving experience or a persistent sense that there is a certain course or direction that we have to take in life can appear to be "God's will."

Hence the crucial question: How do you recognize the difference between "God's will" and an activated complex? How do we distinguish between God's will and a spiritual or psychological wound, or deeply ingrained conditioning that has been awakened, since any of these can overwhelm one's consciousness with emotion?

A complex in us rooted in a subculture in which we have grown up tends to enforce compliance with the values, beliefs, and practices of that subculture. If we feel at odds with aspects of that subculture, we can easily feel guilty. Vivian has told how she felt, especially in Africa.

We have other complexes that are more individual but arise when we cannot affirm our innate wholeness. When these complexes get triggered, several consequences follow:

We don't feel like ourselves; it's as if something has gotten into us.
We behave in a less adapted manner.
Our thinking becomes "black and white": "if you're not with me, then you're against me."
Our capacity for empathy for others tends to disappear.
Other people are to blame for our level of upset and distress.

Complexes typically have a history rooted in the individual's life experiences, often painful experiences from childhood and adolescence. Vivian has gone to some lengths to explain this for her own life.

"God's will," however, has more the sense of being called, being summoned. Such an experience can resemble the Christian Apostle Paul's encounter on the road to Damascus. But more often, it seems to me, Samuel's experience, whether auditory or in image and feeling, characterizes what many people experience.

> As young a boy, Samuel served Eli in the temple. Three times in the night, Samuel heard his name called. Twice he went to Eli. "Here I am. You called me."
> Eli told the boy, "I did not call; go back and lie down." Eli was an old man. The third time Samuel heard his name called, he again went to Eli.
> This time Eli realized that the Lord was calling. So Eli told Samuel, "Go and lie down, and if he calls you, say, 'Speak, Lord, for your servant is listening.'"
> So Samuel went and lay down in his place.
> The Lord came and stood there, calling as at the other times, "Samuel! Samuel!"
> Then Samuel said, "Speak, for your servant is listening" (1 Sam. 3–10) (KJV).

"God's will" may sound old fashioned, perhaps even a bit embarrassing to some twenty-first-century ears. C. G. Jung—whose discoveries, life work, and wisdom influence my thinking—pointed to the fact that people have always and everywhere believed in some sort of Higher Power, often expressed as "God's will." "Psychologically," Jung wrote in a letter, "the 'Will of God' appears in your inner experience in the form of a superior deciding power, to which you may give various names like instinct, fate, unconscious, faith, etc."[56]

Jung insisted he was an empirical scientist, working with facts. He strenuously rejected the accusation that he was a mystic. The experience of a Higher Power is a *psychological* fact, he repeatedly said, that can and does often transcend any denomination or tradition.

"People of the Book"[57]—Jews, Christians, and Muslims—refers to the Hebrew Scriptures, the Christian New Testament, and the Koran for guidance as to God's will. Followers of other faiths have their scriptures and traditions as well. I believe it to be true that followers of these kinds of traditions believe that God revealed the truths contained in scripture to special people, often called prophets.

Jung said that since people have held onto scriptures for centuries, there probably is some value in them[58]. *But revelation continues.* Women and men still experience these even today in dreams and visions and numinous experiences. The revelations recorded in the spiritual traditions and the revelations of contemporary individuals confront us with a major challenge: When to follow the tradition? When to follow what is revealed to me?

A shared ethical foundation underlies all the great spiritual traditions: Don't do to others what you don't want them to do to you. The Golden Rule in its many variations provides a basic test.[59] However, when I follow "the call" coming to me as guidance from my dreams and visions and the sense of what suits me and what doesn't, other people can feel hurt. Vivian was in this plight when she had to follow the path she recognized as authentically hers.

The twentieth-century psychologist Erik H. Erikson addressed this dilemma when he wrote: "For if the simplest moral rule is not to do to another what you would not wish to have done to you, the ethical rule of adulthood is to do to others what will help them, even as it helps you, to grow"[60]. With his ethical rule of adulthood, Erikson validates the innate drive in each human being to become authentically oneself. In the depths of her despair, Vivian heard the call to authentic selfhood. Following the call took tremendous courage. Following the call cost her mightily, but—in the course of time—she grew into the person she really could be.

But what about the others in Vivian's life? How does following Erikson's ethical rule of adulthood help them to grow? By not following the Golden Rule, they were hurt when Vivian did follow Erikson's admonition. Vivian's actions challenged them in at least two ways: Honor the innate potential in me! Honor the reality that you and I are alike in many ways, but also, and importantly, different in significant ways. What suits you doesn't always suit me. Then the second big one: have the courage to honor what in you calls you most persistently. Honor your call.

We see the most fundamental level of personal revelation in Vivian's experience: "I ached to know myself without regard for what I was taught, but no one else would allow it, and I didn't know how to do it on my own. It was too frightening. Even when I could finally act on my own behalf, I was too conditioned to think poorly of myself to begin the process." *Here, the revelation comes as the ache to know herself.*

I know no more eloquent words than those of C. G. Jung with which to affirm Vivian's path and her Meology. Continuing the letter cited above, Jung wrote:

"the psychological criterion of the "Will of God" is forever the dynamic superiority. It is the factor that finally decides when all is said and done. It is essentially something you cannot know beforehand. You only know it after the fact. You only learn it slowly in the course of your life. You have to live thoroughly and very consciously for many years in order to understand what your will is and what Its will is. If you learn about yourself and if eventually you discover more or less who you are, you also learn about God, and who he is. In applying the moral code (which in itself is a commendable thing), you can prevent even the divine decision, and then you go astray. So try to live as consciously, as conscientiously, and as completely as *possible* and learn who you are and who or what it is that ultimately decides."[61]

When you choose to follow what energizes and fascinates you—your individual call—even though other people may not understand or support you, you venture onto the path you have to take. Becoming real is full of false starts, wrong turns, and dead ends. Don't give up! It's worth the effort! The winding path does lead to the goal. The reward is being really you. Know who you are. Be who you are. Tell others who you are. Be.

*E*very time I read what Dr. Matthews has written I feel my feet touching a solid foundation that I can trust and live from—like a pair of shoes that truly fit my feet, as he suggests. I believe Dr. Matthews is talking about knowing ourselves based on our individually unique preferences. ("Pre-references" if you can tolerate another word split.) Preferences perhaps prebuilt into our psyches that set the boundaries between "me" and "you." I call it "greatness," and we each bring it with us into life. We can't help it, but we can lose it unless we make a conscious choice to become it.

Knowing and respecting our inclinations is vital to defining ourselves as that unique individual that each of us is. It's "this little light of mine" that I allow to shine.

In the touching romantic comedy *Runaway Bride*[62], Julia Roberts's character, Maggie Carpenter, is a woman who has very little self-awareness. She's engaged to Coach Bob Kelly (played by Christopher Meloni), a man who believes he knows what's best for her—even the way she should eat eggs. I laughed, but I got it. She couldn't say "I do" to a marriage partner until she could say it to herself. Aha! The Vow to Myself!

When we allow other people's opinions to matter more than our own preferences, we fade; if our standard response to a person's question about our preferences is "It doesn't matter—whatever you want," we become faintly visible ghosts of our purest selves. We must each live from our own vital center or we lose ourselves, and that, according to *Death by Roses*, is hell—to dissolve into other people's opinions of how our lives should be lived so that we vanish.

The gift of knowing our personal proclivities comes only through spending time with ourselves, respecting our priorities, and treating ourselves with the respect that comes from believing that we each make a difference.

Section B

THE THREE WONDERS OF MY RELATIONSHIP
TO MY MOST INTIMATE PARTNER

Fifteen

THE FOURTH WONDER OF THE INNER WORLD:
MY PARTNER—MY MIRROR

*I am in exactly the relationship I need to be, for
reasons I may have yet to discover. If I don't like what
I find in my most intimate relationship, I can resolve
what's causing my discomfort in my inner world.*

—VIVIAN PROBST

*Anyone who becomes deeply important to us is, by that
very fact, replaying a crucial role from our own past. In
fact, this is how people become important to us...our
bond in intimate relationships is often fashioned from
the ancient and twisted consequences of our childhood or
of former relationships...People who become important
to us play supporting roles in our daily drama.*

—DR. DAVID RICHO[63]

In my brother's eye, there is my own soul. In my friend's smile, there is my own humor. In my neighbor's sorrow, there is my own loss.

—U. S. Andersen[64]

Poor Art and Mae Rose McElroy! As they faced their relationship issues, neither could imagine that they were together for any good reason. Neither of them believed in or wanted a divorce—they were too stubborn to admit defeat. Their two boys were grown; they were respected in the community; they had survived Art's affair. Life was predictable; they knew what to expect from each other. As long as Art smoked in the barn and left Mae Rose alone, they were making it through life.

It wasn't that they hadn't loved each other—they could look back at the early years of their marriage and see that they had been more optimistic about their lives, perhaps even excited, as they looked forward to the future. The future had arrived, and it was nowhere near what they had hoped; they blamed each other.

Watching Art and Mae Rose work through their relationship in the story and then learning THIS caused these two discoveries to collide into a startling new look at my marriage. I thought I married Tom for love—and I did—but what if THIS is part of the real reason, *that Tom reflects me to myself? I am in exactly the relationship I need to be for reasons I may have yet to discover.*

Over the course of a committed relationship, we discover new things, and we are changed by them. To look at my most intimate partner and say, "This is who you are, and I can't live with that," is to render ourselves ignorant of what is true about our own selves as well. Instead of owning that we are reflecting each other as we journey to the discovery of our truest selves through the Law of Reflection, we become arrogant judges.

It is always best to work on who we ourselves are becoming rather than focusing on what we believe about someone else—unless our lives are at risk, of course. We can't know anything about others except for what they are reflecting back to us as information for our own growth.

To accuse another is to accuse ourselves. (I know. I don't like that, either.) We are always changing; what or how I am today is not fixed. The more I focus on my inner world and become the radiant being I am discovering myself to be, the more others will radiate my own transformation back to me. If I understand that my inner world is reflecting outward, I will be cautious to judge—replacing that with patience, compassion, and love. As I grow, so does my relationship with others.

*O*h! If we could step back and see how almost impossibly miraculous it is that two egg/sperm combinations came to life and decided to party together to create each of the two people that would be born. Think about how each of us traveled through time and space into the same general vicinity and somehow found each other. It's worth a brief "Wow! Gosh! Holy crap!"

I am always stunned with joy when a couple tells me how they met. It is *always* a miracle and, I believe, purposeful. The same miracle happened for Tom and me, and it's been so good for all of us to go back to that marker together and say, "Wow!"

What if part of my attraction to Tom is for THIS—that this incredible man who loves and cherishes me can also piss me off from time to time so that I am continually cleaning up my inner world, which makes my outer world sparkle more?

What if that was part of the reason we married—so that we could be available to reflect each other and to love each other out of our inner wounds into the people our hearts long to become?

What if you don't complete me—you reflect me? The more I work with THIS, the more excited I become.

(If you can't bear to stay in a relationship, there are ways to physically separate before leaving it altogether. I expand more on this in Chapter 19.)

If any of this is true, what about the marriage I left behind? What about the relationship vows that I didn't fulfill with my first husband? Here again I turn to the fictional story I was given. (You don't have to believe any of *Death by Roses*—it's fiction. But I love the ideas that came to me as I was writing, and since I don't have any other basis on which to know what the next life will be like, fiction works for me. See what you think.)

Death by Roses suggests that just because we end a relationship legally on earth, those watching over us don't feel the slightest need to alter anything at all in higher realms. Is it possible that what we missed in this lifetime will show up in the next one?

What if 'till death do us part' is a myth?

What if relationships don't end when we die or divorce?

I got the sense that relationships may come and go on earth, but it's entirely possible that the energy that is me and the energy that is you, the person I did not stay married to in this lifetime, will meet up again if we need to—if there's any unfinished business between us. It is my honor in this lifetime to have been part of your life; it is now my privilege to continue my journey with another person.

The next wonder of the inner world will suggest that any issues within me that I did not resolve in my prior relationship will not go away when I leave it. Oh no! I brought everything that was still mine to resolve into my marriage to Tom. Maybe that's why I loved living alone for six years—there was no mirror staring back at me. It was more peaceful.

That's when I got it—all my old wounds still needed attention. Crap! They weren't going to disappear just because I had remarried. Damn! It took my second marriage for me to realize that. (Also, it took a thorough read of Byron Katie's *Loving What Is*[65], which so completely changed my understanding of the purpose of relationships.) What Tom and I were experiencing wasn't his fault—it wasn't my fault—these were my same old wounds begging to be healed. That was all, and all it took was THIS.

Sixteen

The Fifth Wonder of the Inner World:
If You're Saying That I Really Want This, You're Wrong!

*Who I am in a relationship with is less important
than who I am being in that relationship.*

—Vivian Probst

*The only time we suffer is when we believe a thought
that argues with what is…wanting reality to be
different than it is, is hopeless. When the mind is
perfectly clear, what is, is what we want.*

—Byron Katie

"What is, is what we want," says Katie.[66] Does that surprise you? It did me! It's not that it doesn't matter at all—it's that we attracted who we did for a reason, and I want to get what I need from that relationship before I move on. Because moving on can bring me more pain if I don't do the inner work that my current relationship was intended for.

Don't we want to be married to our soul mate—the one we're supposed to be with rather than a "stand-in?" How do we know the difference—or is there one? Isn't that why we often leave one marriage for another?

What if "the one I'm with" is my soul mate for right now, and I'm looking in "all the wrong places" except at what he or she reflects to me?

While it's not wrong to leave, at least in my opinion, the real question is, why am I leaving?

Do I just need to get away? All of us need alone time (even and perhaps because we are in such a close relationship when married). Some short breaks might be a good idea to test that premise before I call for the moving van.

Am I looking to a different relationship to make me feel better about myself? (Newsflash from THIS: I can do it for myself.)

Have I attracted a different person because I'm ready for that one? It's possible. However, I think most divorce counselors would say that the person you meet who takes you away from a relationship is not necessarily the one, if you know what I mean. I shudder to imagine that the first man I dated after my marriage was over was the one I would spend the rest of my life with. Anyone agree?

When I married Tom, I had a true and genuine affection for him. I loved him. The week after, I wasn't so sure. (I hope you smile—It took more than a week for me to question whether or not I'd done the right thing in marrying him, but I did get there and questioned myself over and over and over.)

What happens to a relationship over time is the focus of the Fifth Wonder of the Inner World. I'm not qualified to advise other people about their relationships, but I absolutely agree with Katie in her book.

Already fascinated by quantum science, I found that Katie's approach to relationships opened the door for me to look deeper into my relationship with Tom and to find my own self-judgments and criticisms at work. Using her "Four Question" process, I investigated not only my marriage but *every* relationship that was causing me to suffer. It was then that I discovered a pattern—a consistency that drove me to accept a truth I had not realized before that time. *I was my own worst enemy, <u>and</u> the people showing up in my life were there to help me see that, so that I could make it stop because I was the one who had created it.*

While *I Was a Yo-Yo Wife* focuses on intimate relationships, THIS applies to all kinds of relationships. In my case, I wasn't just having problems with my marriage. My issues were also evident in the consulting business I owned and the people I hired, who were as hard on me as I felt Tom was (and just as wrong and blameworthy, in my opinion, as it was back then). There was, at last, no getting away from realizing the major role I played in setting up my world to work against me.

It is with that understanding that I share what I learned about this Fifth Wonder of the World. *No one is going to resolve my inner issues but me.* With my whole heart, I believe that there's a higher purpose to an intimate relationship, and THIS is it.

I absolutely love how Katie works with people to help us see the mirror that the person we most deeply resent (and that can be an intimate partner) can shine the brightest light on what will only bless us, once we allow ourselves to see it.

To leave Tom would have meant starting over with another person (perhaps), or living without that type of mirror. (I'm not saying that people who live alone have no reflectors—they just don't live and sleep with them. Others can decide whether or not that's an advantage.) I decided to stick with the one I was already with and take care of the issues that showed up between us.

It's true that I sometimes felt emotionally abused (ignored) during my second marriage; I didn't realize that I was particularly sensitive because of what I had experienced in my early childhood. My upbringing, my first marriage—and my entire culture—had robbed me of any sense that I played a meaningful role in life or that I was worthy of love.

During those precious, growing years between marriages, I had grown past that unworthy sense of myself, but I hadn't tested it inside a relationship. Oh la la! I became incredibly touchy if Tom rolled his eyes at something I said or if he spoke to me in a commanding voice, suggesting that I had better do what he wanted.

Can you understand how this could happen? Once I had broken out of the religious society that perpetrated those painful beliefs that I was an unworthy sinner and that I was to submit myself to my husband in a way that did not honor me, I had begun to see myself differently; I enjoyed my independence and the thrill of finding respect and purpose in the world.

My second marriage posed threats to my new sense of myself. What shocked me was that when we had conflict, I automatically reverted to my old patterns! I felt small and invisible; I was afraid of Tom's anger. This was the woman I *had* been—not the woman I now was. I didn't understand why I wasn't coping as the independent adult woman I now knew myself to be. It was frightening, and sometimes as I felt myself losing ground, I left.

Learning THIS was critical to my growth beyond those tendencies, because with acute accuracy, Tom was able to reflect back to me what was going on inside of me. When we weren't getting along, he brought all my old terror out into the open.

Only when I learned THIS—that the whole reason for these occurrences was to help me see how deeply encoded my life still was with self-loathing—did I learn to be free by drenching myself with love.

My husband's outbursts ("as few as they were," he would say) reflected my own; his fears mirrored mine. He was showing me all of this so that I could release it. Imagine!

In the beginning of this book, I promised I would say something about Tom's inability to remember these heartrending circumstances as well as I do. I believe there could be something very interesting at play here—besides the fact that he's a man. Is it possible that my partner doesn't recall events like these because they were merely reflectors that were operating through him? Could these be unconscious to him and coming through for only me to see? It's a frightening, provocative possibility. I've seen it at work enough times to consider the possibility that the energy coming through to shine light on something that it wants to reach in and pull out of me has a particularly bad habit that could include a veiled memory for the transmitting person.

Here's an example of something that happened to me that caused me to consider the possibility. I was in Washington, DC, attending an affordable-housing conference. It was typical for me to speak on several panels at these conferences and to share dinner at the end of the days with folks from different states and agencies. I knew many of these people quite well, and I treasured the opportunity to spend quality time around a dinner table with them.

This particular night, a man I didn't know joined our group and proceeded to be quite vulgar to me. Since he was seated directly across from me at the table and I didn't want to offend the group, I did my best to keep the conversation neutral and to include other people sitting around us in conversation.

At one point he left to use the bathroom. When he came back to the table, he was completely different. He approached me, leaned over toward me, and said in a warning tone, "Do not pursue the research you are planning; everything you need to know will be provided. Do no research." Then he disappeared.

He didn't know me; he didn't know that I was beginning research on a book I was going to write about a historic event—a mystery from the 1600s that had never been resolved. (When this five-volume series comes out, it will probably be titled "The Woman Who Forgot Who She Was"). While it was a gruff encounter, I understood that I had to solve the mystery from my own imagination; that research would destroy my ability to do that. Writing *Death by Roses* interrupted my focus on that mystery. What I know for sure is that my imagination is still busy putting the pieces together. I've learned to be patient even though I am almost dizzy with anticipation.

I've come to believe that the kind of unwarranted intensity I observed in this man and that I have seen in Tom from time to time—completely out of character for him—originates from an energetic source that is beyond human comprehension. When Tom is showing high intensity about something, I've learned to pay attention. Without being conscious of it, he's probably wielding a laser-beam focus on something of extremely high importance for me. I've learned not to distance myself at these moments. Rather, I lean in to get clarity.

That means it's important to pay attention to my partner most intently when we are in conflict, which is now extremely rare.

When I look with greater weight and focus at who my partner is being in relation to me—that is, when I place greater and more critical emphasis on how my partner is behaving—I lose the benefit for which this relationship was created. In any relationship, particularly with an intimate other, it is the greatest privilege to see what that person is reflecting that is true inside of me rather than judging who *he or she* is by their behavior. If I have set the boundaries about what is tolerable and acceptable to me and I require it to be followed by others, what do I do when they behave outside my acceptable boundaries? Before I ignore or discredit them, it's a worthy exercise to look for what they might be showing me about my own self.

When I start to think that someone else would be a better partner for me, it is important to be absolutely clear and free to make that decision. However, if I have not taken seriously the reflection of my current intimate partner for my own highest evolution, then discarding that mirror works against me. It is better to clear my negative reaction to another—to acknowledge it as my reaction to myself—rather than to change partners.

This is the "mote and beam" premise that is spoken of in the Bible (as referenced earlier) and by great philosophers throughout all time.

Imagine how much more exciting life can be if we accept that our partners, with all their human inadequacies that drive us out of our minds, are serving THIS great purpose. It's better than a reality show!

Seventeen

The Sixth Wonder of the Inner World: *If Ever I Would Leave You*

I can leave a relationship as long as I realize that I take my own unresolved issues with me and that they will follow me until I allow THIS to transform and release them.

—Vivian Probst

This is the end of blame, of playing victim. Anything that tags along with me after I leave an externally challenging situation is mine to deal with. That was tough for me to integrate. I was so good at blaming others; I knew how to play the victim perfectly.

Wise counsel at the Women's Center after my divorce first set me on the right course. After I lamented my past to my gentle counselor, Anne B. (different from the Anne of *Relationship Rules of a Happy Woman*), she told me, "Vivian, you're an adult now. Whatever happened in the past is over. It's your choice how to live your life going forward." I didn't believe her back then—not like I do now. I had to test the concept for, oh, say, a few decades.

I couldn't completely grasp what my counselor told me at the time, but it got into my psyche. Every time I watched it play out somewhere or when I saw it come up as I went through Meology, I became more conscious. But like Anne had said, it is always my choice, and sometimes it was easier to hide from being responsible by blaming others. Not really, of course, because sooner or later, I would learn that it wasn't helping me. But life takes time; learning to know and adore ourselves is worth every ounce of energy and every minute we put into it.

Some of us are stubborn or deeply wounded; some of us have to have the truth handed to us on a plate of broken glass. Pain is a harsh teacher—sometimes it's the only way we wake up from our old patterns. So what? Sooner or later it comes to us, whether we get it in our next life like Mae Rose or we get it the day after tomorrow. The year 2008 was my time to learn that Anne had been right all those years ago. But I hadn't wallowed in nonexistence during those intervening years—I had unpacked some of my old worn-out beliefs along the way and brought in some new, gorgeous ones; I had experiences that reminded me that I was good and worthy and loved.

But if it's time to leave, it's time to leave. Let's talk about that now.

Five Ways to Leave Your Lover!

In the famous Paul Simon song, "Fifty Ways to Leave Your Lover"[67], only five ways to leave are mentioned, but they are each different and important. I have categorized them as follows:

1. Spontaneous exits: just slip out the back, Jack/ie.
2. Planned retreats: make a new plan, Stan/Ann.
3. Stating our intentions: no need to be coy, Roy/Joy.
4. Taking a longer trip away: back on the bus, Gus/Gustine.
5. Leaving for good: just drop off the key, Lee.

1. Spontaneous Exits: Just Slip Out the Back, Jack/ie

I'm not proud about leaving Tom as much as I did and often without notice, but when you've gotta go, you've gotta go. Perhaps sharing my experience and what I learned will help more of us to have the courage and self-respect to take a time-out when it's called for.

In the beginning, I found Tom's energy overwhelming. He was always working on something, while I often found I still needed space for the quiet reflection I had become accustomed to in my years alone. A couple needs to honor differences. As much as I wanted to be like Tom, I wasn't. Sometimes I just had to find space for myself.

I would often wait until I felt overwhelmed—like I just had to get out for a while and *right now*. That meant I'd just take off, not always knowing where I was going or for how long. I'd find a hotel room, lock myself inside, and catch my breath. I learned that all I needed was some "me" time. After a few hours, an overnight, or a weekend, I'd feel restored.

Tom would hunt me down, and I'd talk to him about what was going on. If we'd had an argument and needed to clear the air, I felt as if I could do that more safely from a distance than in person. Tom is a brilliant debater. Unaccustomed as I was to being heard, much less expressing myself in an argument, I vanished until my feet were on the ground again.

Too often I still see women who don't take time for themselves. They martyr themselves, and the world suffers the result. It might be true that for some women, there might not be that need. I know women who are so content in their roles as wives and mothers that they can't wait to plan for the next birthday party or craft day with the kids. If that's a woman's Meology, that's awesome.

For every woman I know who cherishes motherhood to the point of total absorption, I know two women who would take an afternoon or a day or two to regroup if they felt that they could. On the surface there's the guilt/cost factor. It might cost money to be away, or my husband might object to handling the kids alone. On the inside I wonder if, like my own experience in the beginning, we are afraid of time alone because it will require us to give our hearts and souls attention—attention that could point to some orphans that need us just as much as our external family does.

It can be scary for us to think of being alone even for a short amount of time. It feels easier to stay home, but it's not. When a woman needs time to nurture herself and she doesn't take it, I believe there's a sacrifice going on that can breed resentment and hostility.

In *The Artist's Way*, Julia Cameron[68] deals with this by having students of her methods take an evening once a week to do something solely for themselves. If we don't honor the calling of our inner world, we pay the price, whatever it might be. "Blocking," she says, "is essentially an issue of faith. Rather than trust our intuition, our talent, our skill, or our desire, we fear where our creator is taking us with this creativity. Rather than paint, write, dance, audition, and see where it takes us, we pick up a block. Blocked, we know who we are and what we are: unhappy people. Unblocked, *we may be something much more threatening—happy. For most of us, happy is terrifying, unfamiliar, out of control, and too risky!*"

I meet women at the hair salon, basking in the pedicure and manicure process, looking at magazines, and working a little bit of "me time" into their lives. A commute to work can provide that as well. Finding time to unplug is less difficult if we want it—if we are not afraid to have it. A daily exercise and/or meditation routine or a cup of coffee or a glass of wine with a friend can be just perfect.

The older we get, the more we need to pay attention to THIS.

In her book from a number of years ago, now called *The Wisdom of Menopause* (or as my linguist mind loves to put it, *men-o-pause*), Dr. Christiane Northrup startled me with her idea that hot flashes could be indications of deep, unmet, soulful needs. Of her own experience, she wrote, "The coming of my hot flashes had signaled another stage in my own midlife reevaluation—a commitment to setting healthier boundaries, to taking better care of myself, to speaking the truth. The change is not simply a collection of physical problems to be 'fixed'…but a mind-body revolution that brings the greatest opportunity for growth since adolescence"[69].

My personal physician, Dr. Rose Kumar, has focused her entire medical career on helping women through this transition. In her book *Becoming Real: Reclaiming Your Health in Midlife*, Kumar talks about menopause as a time for women to reconnect with what she calls the "Feminine Principle." She writes, "It takes courage and endurance to reintegrate the feminine into our relationship with ourselves. This is our holy task through midlife…we must choose to live from our truth and enter the world of the soul"[70].

Menopause is a physical, emotional, and spiritual drama. If we have ignored our inner world before this time, our orphans can get pretty noisy. Even a woman's monthly cycle can bring up wounds begging to be healed. These are powerful times if we treat them with respect. If we ignore them and act as if they are only physical transition points, I believe we lose the gift that's waiting inside the heat, and it will take additional festering for our wounds to get our attention at a later time.

A challenge: Promise yourself that you will set aside two hours a week for yourself. Then do it! (That's 17.1 minutes per day. Say YES to THIS and watch Life support your ability to find time)!

2. Planned Retreats: Make a New Plan, Stan/Ann

I see more and more women going on planned retreats. Whether it's a weekend trip to a nearby town or Vegas, we are giving ourselves permission to take a break with others. It's good; it's fun; women tend to nurture one another. What I hope for is that women will take some of these longer periods of time to be alone with themselves—complete with spa services, a journal, some magazines, and a little extra cash if possible.

Life is never stingy with time or money, but we can be. While I've had my share of financial ups and downs, I've always been taken care of. I agree with Esther Hicks and Abraham and a host of others—depriving ourselves of these types of gifts (i.e., time for myself) can send the wrong message to the universe. If we're not willing to take time for ourselves, can we really expect to be blessed and nurtured?

Like most women, my whole life has been about others. I have always been a giver. I can always find a place to spend money or a charity to give it to. Keeping money for myself has been virtually impossible. It's an orphan that wants my attention. Shortchanging ourselves tells Life that we can do without—that we don't feel worthy of its gifts.

When you're raised to save the world, you don't expect to get rich in the process. The mantra of my family for generations has been to donate generously to mission organizations. When my parents could not go to the mission field because of my mother's health challenges, my father became a doctor. I believe it was the first time anyone in his family for generations had money, and I think he didn't know what to do with it.

I remember living in a spacious home; I recall Dad sitting at the kitchen table balancing his checkbook. I would walk by and ask, "Dad, how much money do you have in the bank?"

He would put his head in his hands and say, "Not a dime, honey, not a dime." It was always gone somewhere.

Life has had much to teach me about money. I don't want to walk down that road in this book, but it is important to honor and respect ourselves. One way we do that is by contributing financially to our joyful well-being.

A challenge: Plan a weekend trip (one or two nights away) for yourself. Take a friend if you're uncomfortable going alone, but promise yourself you will spend at least two hours of each day you are away on yourself.

3. Stating Our Intentions: No Need to Be Coy, RoyJoy

Family time is important, of course, and in today's world, gathering around the dinner table together can take a miracle. Even then, it's vital to our vitality to be open about the time we need for ourselves. It should be part of a conversation and planning discussion. The family should get used to the idea of Mom being away every so often.

My best friend and I have been going away together once or twice a year for over thirty years. When we started, my children were pretty much grown up, while hers were much younger. Getting her husband, Mr. L., excited about Mrs. L. and I going away took time. We started with day-trips, then overnight, then over two nights. Now we can take longer trips because we started with a short amount of time and let it expand.

Oh, the fun we've had! The memories! By taking time for ourselves, we hope both of us have taught our children the value of friendship and taking time.

I've been writing for many years. Every so often, I have to take time alone to complete a task (like I'm doing right now). As a writer, it's true that I can work pretty much anywhere. But I need to clear time for my writing and also for my own growth and nurturing and then for friends and family. Tom will ask, "What about me? I don't see my name mentioned anywhere." It's true. It's easy to take our spouses for granted.

Tom and I need time for us as well. It simply works best if we intend it. Tom and I have to actually spend money on reserving plane tickets to commit ourselves to a vacation! That's a good way to state an intention. Put some money down on it!

If you're a working woman as I have been for over thirty years, getting all of this squeezed into the spaces we have in life can take some doing. That's why we need to make others aware of our intentions—so that they are prepared. Then there's this amazing concept called the universe. I've found that when I need time, it is where I turn to open up what I need. The concept of taking time is a good one. Time is flexible. Whenever we just take it as if it's ours to do whatever we want to with, it says, OK! Everything that's important fits itself in somewhere. What's not important simply disappears.

In 2012, when I was very challenged by the lack of time in life, I took a quantum-physics approach and wrote a short story titled "The TimeMaker's Shop."[71] (When we give up trying to fit everything in and remain open, allowing the universe to organize everything, time becomes a nonissue. When we need it and we know it, we simply take it. Miraculously, everything else readjusts easily, unless we've got an orphan screaming at us. Good thing we know how to deal with orphans!

4. *Taking a Longer Trip Away: Back on the Bus, Gus/Gustina*

At one of the most critical times of our marriage, our counselor suggested we needed time apart. I think it was in 1991, five years into our marriage. Tom went to the YMCA, where he stayed for three months. I stayed at the house.

The rules were that (a) we couldn't talk to each other on the phone; we could only write letters to each other; and (b) we would meet once a week with the counselor.

(The children knew nothing about this—we were able to work around their schedules, and since both of us traveled, it was acceptable to let them think that the other person was out of town.) I'm not sure many counselors recommend this kind of separation, but I was amazed at what I learned about Tom and about myself.

By the time this occurred, Tom and I were in constant conflict; even then, we hated how we were treating each other. I remember a night when my two children were staying over, and my daughter used her stepsister's pillow. Tom had a fit—over a pillow. Can you see how something so small in reality can become so big when we are at odds with ourselves and each other? We both wanted to stop hurting each other. That's why we had separated.

While we were apart, Tom surprised me by becoming a passionate letter writer. Most days when I got home from work, there would be a thick letter waiting for me. He was taking this seriously, as was I.

Our counselor was a kind man, who kept asking us, "Where's the marriage? I see that you really care about each other, but Tom, you're busy with your career, and Vivian, you with yours. Where's the 'we' part of the relationship?"

We didn't have a clue what he was talking about. Both of us supported each other's goals and dreams, which we believed was quite enough. We were both free to travel, and neither of us doubted the other in terms of fidelity. We believed that was what being married meant.

I like to joke that once I met Tom, a sign appeared on my forehead that said Taken (and not the movie version, starring Liam Neeson). There was a lock and seal on my heart, even though I had to run away from it from time to time. No man ever made a pass at me after I met Tom. This love, so evident to others, often eluded us.

While we were separated over that three-month period, the movie *Green Card*[2] had come out; I went to see it alone. Those of you who know the story line will understand why I called Tom, weeping that same night, and asked him to come home. He did. Immediately. If you haven't seen *Green Card*, we highly recommend it. Watching the couple who had married simply for legal purposes actually fall in love and then be forced to be separated helped me to realize what life without Tom would be like. I opted back in.

om and I are sharing very intimate details of our relationship—details about our troubles that very few people ever knew. We're only doing it because of what we learned, and with the hope it might help others. If you think I'm a yo-yo, I won't blame you; I only hope you can see that while I often jumped overboard and swam away, Life made sure there was always a life preserver that brought me home. If we could catch a glimpse of that flotation device now, I believe it would have "T.O.M." printed on it. And it would be attached to a yacht by a strong rope of love.

Should you and your partner separate for a time? Only the two of you and a wise counselor who knows you well can make that decision. We hope that sharing these insights can help. And we hope you remember that once I learned THIS, our relationship issues took on a whole new light.

5. Just Drop Off the Key, Lee, and Set Yourself Free!

Yes, sometimes you have to leave. I left one marriage, so I understand the consequences and benefits of such a decision. If someone ever asks me, "Should I stay, or should I go?" I intend to give them a copy of this book. If what I've learned has any substance to it, the real issue to address is what it is am I not seeing or dealing with in my inner world that is causing this reflection in my outer world.

Relationships can be saved; marriages can be resurrected. But not all of them. The only marriage I saved was mine. The question that each of us must ask and answer from our souls is, *Do I want to try? Am I willing?* You see, I was the only one 'working on my marriage', which was really about working on my own self. Tom was busy taking care of life from his perspective which wasn't working for me. I chose and I worked intently on my own life issues. Now I see how that saved my marriage.

I've previously stated my opinion that one reason to end a relationship is abuse—physical, emotional or otherwise; it becomes urgent to stop the suffering—even more so if there are children involved. I've also listed some additional and perhaps somewhat intangible forms of abuse that we often put up with because we don't see them as abusive or we think 'this is as good as it gets'.

I can also attest to my personal experience that leaving does not in and of itself end the internal root cause of the abuse. That's what my second marriage taught me. By taking care of my inner world, my marriage changed.

It would be uncomfortable for me as an unlicensed individual to discuss reasons to leave a relationship. But I know I am not alone in believing that one person can change a relationship (for better or worse). I'm a fan of Mort Fertel, his blog and his books.[73] It's almost like we're connected telepathically because we are so in tune with our philosophies. I'd invite you to sign up for his free subscription services and get involved in some of his "Marriage Fitness" courses if you want an official guide to assist you in dealing with any obstacles you are facing in your relationship.

Coping with Regret

Before concluding this chapter, I want to talk about the issue of regret because it comes up as in the natural process of letting go. I have already shared that my first marriage ended because I had to leave a way of life that no longer served me. I had married into a belief system in order to keep myself obedient to it. When I could no longer stay, it meant leaving everything.

Of course, I have regrets about that. Of course, others were affected by my decision. Yet I would not change anything except to say that I wish I'd known THIS sooner; I wish I'd given myself permission to move toward my passionate interests my whole life. But then—and this is where regrets get tricky—I wouldn't have the wonderful children and grandchildren I do. I can't imagine life without them. So, honestly, I wouldn't change anything.

In my opinion, regrets are the deepest wounds we carry and the hardest to heal because we keep picking at them. They are the orphans that don't want to leave and the ones we must patiently extract because our true power is trapped inside. Every time we regret something (notice the *re* syllable), we create more pain over the same event. We can't regret our way into a wonderful life, so it's very important to spend extra time in the Pool of Unconditional Love when one of these shows up. And hang on to them tightly until they transform, because they're slippery!

If it's time to move on, let's do it with all the love and compassion we can offer to ourselves, our children, and those we leave behind. We might spend hours at the Pool of Unconditional Love—our wounds may keep us awake at night, but drenching everyone with love will ultimately prevail. (I also keep a squirt gun of pink loving energy from the Pool handy, just in case an attack of regret surprises me).

Section C

The Wonder of My Relationship to the Source of Life

Eighteen

The Seventh Wonder of the Inner World: *My Relationship to the Source of Life*

*I am deeply loved and connected to the Source of Everything
that lives and breathes through me, whether I believe it or not.
That Source is profoundly interested in me
and cares about me to the nth degree.*

—Vivian Probst

It's easy to want to skip this part, especially if your mind is screaming, "What hogwash!" I would hate to lose readers because I might offend your beliefs. I include it because love, however we define it, is the key to teaching ourselves compassion. I know because I'm still learning every day how much I am loved by Life.

I had no concept of this kind of love growing up. God was a stern man with rules that I, as a woman, could never satisfy. Yes, I believed that Jesus died for my sins, but I couldn't get past that to the love part. There was no role model for me to look at and see love—only judgment. I believe there are millions of people who have had no concept of love, but I also believe that it is inherent in us to recognize love when it shows up, since we come from it.

THIS put me in touch with love in a way I had not known before. Even now I return to the Pool of Unconditional Love just to feel it wash over me again and again. My life has taken on an entirely new and special joy. I've learned that it's best to stay near that pool because life on earth can overwhelm any sense of wonder I possess. Practicing is also good for a marriage.

Those of us who weren't loved in the earliest times of our lives find the concept of a divine Source of Love almost unimaginable, and it's almost impossible to share love if we don't know it for ourselves. The beauty of THIS is that as I take time to journey inward, the layers of old pain that used to keep me from recognizing my original beauty and the Source that wants me to see it become thinner. Life teaches me how to love who I truly am—a spark of living, breathing divinity that overflows into life when it is set free.

Long before a child can grasp the religious concept that God is Love, its definition has been branded into the infant's fragile and tender vibrational receptors. We know how to define it; we know how it feels before we can say the word. Or we know what Not Love feels like.

Suffering was my first association with the idea of love, and it became more acute as I grew up. It was part of God's plan; we were sinners—pain and suffering were our birthrights. From my earliest memories, I knew that my mother suffered. When I was old enough to begin to understand, she often told me of her anguish. Most of it was centered on what my father was or wasn't doing, so that blame became part of the recipe of love. If you loved, you suffered; you focused on the source of your suffering, which was always external. You grieved; you blamed; you did your best to change the other person.

We would occasionally sit together as a family for a meal; it was rare for Dad to be home that early in the evening—his doctoring life was so full of emergencies for other people that dinnertime at home often turned into Mom dissolving in tears because the man she loved simply wasn't there enough. Far too often, she took her rage out on her children. The concept of a loving relationship with Life was quite foreign to me. I followed that definition of love in my first marriage because it was all I knew, and I felt utterly unloved.

When Life showed me THIS--as I adored and healed my inner wounds with compassion, only then was I able to see a new framework establish love for myself and Tom inside our marriage. THIS taught me to cherish my husband instead of railing on him for what I perceived as his inadequacies.

As I shared in Chapter 6, blaming others for my suffering was easy, but it never produced the results I ached for. If I am lost in my pain, I can't possibly express love for another person. The other person can never fill me up enough. I can reach out for love, but it's like trying to grasp a cloud. I can need love, but no one else can fulfill that need; I can leave to find love somewhere else, but it is a futile search.

Once I began my own inner-world journeys to the Pool of Unconditional Love with the pieces of myself that I had refused to care for—once I began to care for myself in this way, I found how easy it was to love my husband *and* to believe in a divine source of love that was interested in me. Only then did I understand love for the first time. It made me giddy and still does.

When I began to experience this love inside myself, for myself, I grew roots that anchored, stabilized, and nurtured me. It braced me for the times when contrast demanded that I see what love was not. Without this contrast, I would never have known what love is. Imagine the thrill of the discovery of love! I grew roots that allowed my branches to extend beyond my inner world to the outside.

I believe that all the rage and suffering in the world today stems from a lack of self-love—that war and greed and terrorism are expressions of outrage from the rage we cannot conquer within. That's a strong statement, and if I were the only person in the world who found this to be true, I would be very lonely. But through all the ages of time and space, the message of a divine Source of Love has been the primary quest of every human being.

It is only deep love—a love relentless in its pursuit of my happiness and highest good—that can transform me. How can it be that Life cares so deeply for me that it will always extend the highest and best quality of compassion for me as it seeks to bring me home to my authentic self? Such a journey necessarily requires that Life give back to me the most accurate reflection of my inner reality. It cannot pretend otherwise without defrauding me of clarity.

Therefore, it is with gratitude that I accept what is being reflected to me by my most intimate partner. In the embrace of Life's love for me, truth sets me free by its transparency. I am careful to respect the vibrational accuracy of what I'm observing because something inside me heals.

When we feel safe inside love, we automatically share it; we can't help it. Once I learned THIS, I experienced that sharing for the first time. Tom has been a primary focus of that love for many years, and I know that love is reciprocated. After all, we reflect one another. Yes?

I have learned how to express the kindness of love in my relationship with Tom. Sometimes I have to stop and ask myself, *Who is this woman who used to scowl when her husband got home because of her growing list of 'Things That My Husband Does Wrong'? How did that turn into the growing list of 'Things That My Husband Does Right'? How did I transform from complaining and nagging to loving and appreciating?*

My guess is that Tom has had to adjust to this new format as well. Once we are sensitized to a particular behavior, any change causes us to become suspicious. It takes time to show another person what has changed so profoundly inside ourselves.

After so many years of marriage, Tom and I still find unique ways to express our love for each other. One of our rituals is leaving notes for each other if we are going to be separated overnight. Sticky notes appear on our mirrors, under our pillows, inside cabinet doors, or on refrigerator jars. When we are home together, we kiss each other—a lot. We say "thank you" to each other. My favorite time of day is when we are both home together in the early evening. We go to the bar in our home—a special place—and meet just like we would if we went out to a bar. We open a bottle of wine, and we talk. Personally, this intimate time means as much to me as making love with our bodies. Talking is making love with our souls.

Tom buys me roses and brings me chocolate and cigars. He takes care of me in ways I sometimes don't even notice; I hope I do the same for him. If there's something that bothers me, I take it inside first to study it, resolve it with unconditional love, and get the blessing wrapped inside it before I make an issue of it with Tom. Often I don't even have to bring up the problem, because it disappears into love. I feel respected and loved. We laugh a lot.

*E*arlier in this book, I mentioned the new perspective I have on erroneously thinking that my spouse can have a problem that has nothing to do with me. In an intimate relationship, I don't believe there's any such thing as "your problem." We are too close and too reflective to be that separate. If it's a problem for my spouse, there's something for me to know. Because of what THIS has taught me, I pay attention. Here's a recent example of how that works with THIS.

For quite some time, Tom has been dealing with an issue that has been difficult to resolve. As soon as I became aware of his struggle, and especially when I realized it was intensifying, it became a "hit" for me. Tom was dealing with his issue; at the same time, since it was reflecting into my world, there was probably something in my inner world trying to get my attention as well. I went inside to find a vibrational match.

There are two clues that I look for to know if it's time for me to take a tour of Planet Me: if something in the external world—particularly in my spouse's—has (a) an enduring, repetitive resilience (it won't go away, no matter what) and (b) an increasing intensity (it gets worse and worse or harder and harder). Tom's experience had these qualities. It suggested that there might be a reflective quality for me to pay attention to. There was. Acting as if it was only his problem was not the answer. I knew better.

For about the same amount of time as Tom had been trying to resolve this matter, I had been working on getting my precious novel, *Death by Roses*, into the public eye. It wasn't going as well as I had hoped, and I was feeling some significant and deepening disappointment, which I had been ignoring.

I was doing everything I knew to do to get the word out. I loved this novel; it had won an award; I was still so sure it would be a hit. The fact that fifty thousand new titles came out every year didn't faze me. But it brought me to grief on more than one occasion. I suffered as the world shows a stunning lack of interest. *What was I doing wrong? Why was this happening?*

I expected the magic of writing this novel to spill out and overflow to a large audience right away. This wasn't the case. I had been struggling with this inside myself when the issue that Tom was struggling with came to a head. Aha! It was time to go inside my own world to see if I had another orphan to deal with. It took all of three minutes.

Inside the Orphanage, which is still a very large place with lots of rooms (many of them are now vacant and renovated), I wandered up and down hallway after hallway, looking for my elusive orphan. I was pleased that so many of my issues were resolved; I also knew that some of the big ones were still hiding out; they weren't particularly interested in coming home to me and jumping into the Pool of Unconditional Love. I think they were more interested in lynching me.

All I needed to do was identify the source of pain that I had been feeling—the vibrational match. I knew immediately what it was about—my creativity and the intense pain of my beloved book not being seen by the world. I could ignore it no longer.

On the positive side, reviews of the book were very, very good; I often heard of people who had shared the book with someone else who had shared it with someone else, and people were loving it. That helped, but nothing could heal the deep pain I was feeling. That was the clue that it was time to find this languishing orphan and bring it home—which proved to be a difficult task.

When I finally found this one, it was lying down with its back turned to me; its flesh looked like mincemeat, as if it had been whipped mercilessly. And it was large—a huge man.

I walked up to him and said, "Hey." (I felt silly after I said that, but it was the opening that came to me.)

He did not respond. Perhaps I was being too casual. "Hello," I said again. Same silent treatment.

"You look pretty messed up; I'd like to help you out and get you fixed up," I said.

No response, not even a twitch. Was this guy dead? I put my hand on his shoulder.

"Do not touch me!" His voice, coming from the depths of his being, shook me to my core. "Do not ever touch me!" He didn't turn to look at me—he didn't move at all.

The shock was incredible. "I only—"

"Get out! Get out of here! You've done enough damage already!" His back was still turned to me.

This was my planet. I knew I wasn't going to leave; that didn't mean I knew what to do. So I sat and waited for an idea. "I'm not leaving here without you," I said.

"Then make yourself comfortable somewhere else. Leave me alone! I mean it! I hate you!"

This tense situation lasted long enough that I actually thought I'd come up against the toughest orphan ever, and that indeed, I might never be able to leave. (Remember, in real time, about one minute had elapsed.)

It took longer to get through to this orphan than any of the others I had ever encountered. Eventually I got that this was my "creative self" orphan— the part of my creativity that I subjected to constant pressure to be successful. (No wonder it wasn't talking to me.)

In my growing-up years, I had been raised to save the world from hell; what lingered after I left that belief system was an incredible need to save the world from something or anything else. There was this *big* need to prove that my life and work still mattered, even if the focus was no longer on religious salvation.

Once I got this orphan to talk, I learned that while most of the other orphans were actually relieved to see me and had gladly reunited with me, this guy had no desire to ever leave the confines of the Orphanage. He would rather die, and I can't say I blame him.

To lose contact with my creative self-felt like death to me. I renewed my commitment to never harm my creative self again—to always honor it, no matter how the world might see it—or not. I eventually moved into position to hug it exactly where it was, even if I never saw its face or felt its inspiration again—even if it never wanted to play in the Pool of Unconditional Love.

As Tom was dealing with his own situation, I could see myself and the truth this orphan revealed to me. Everything I created, everything I wrote, and everything I taught was loaded with this requirement to succeed beyond my wildest expectations—a backhanded way to find approval that what I was doing was "enough." Since nothing I had ever created had saved the world, this orphan had been the obvious recipient of my enduring rage and frustration.

As far as I know, I'm still lying there, soothing this wound. I had forgotten that creativity doesn't flourish when there's a price tag on its head and impossible expectations it is required to fulfill. Creativity is supposed to be *fun*. Over the course of time, my creativity has returned as if to tell me that I am forgiven, but I must never again supplant its purpose with my own.

Tom had helped me once again—this time through his own struggle.

The reasons I've told this story are threefold: (1) I am still learning, 2) THIS is still an effective tool after all these years, and 3) I want you to know what happened next and how I immediately had the most incredible experience. These experiences are common after I deal with an orphan. For me, it's a constant reminder that Life loves me.

When I came out of this provocative session in which my creativity orphan insisted that I "love my creativity for what it was, not how much money it could finally create for me to vindicate myself," Tom told me that his issue was resolved. He was so relieved, he almost wept. I gave thanks.

I went to sit at my computer and pick up my writing. Then I saw that I had an e-mail from my assistant, indicating that a TV-show producer had seen the *Death by Roses* book cover in a magazine. They wanted to know if TV rights were available, and would we please send them a copy of the book? Boy, oh boy! Both of these events were instantaneous after my visit to the Orphanage. I believe in serendipity. OK, the TV deal didn't go anywhere—yet—but what a big boost to an unknown author!

*E*very time I work though an issue that's causing me pain on the inside of my life, I get an almost instant hit like this. *Every time.* It's as if Life can do something wonderful for me now that I've removed yet another obstacle. Perhaps you can see why I am sold on THIS!

Life taught me a way to take care of my old wounds and transform them. I still visit the Orphanage, perhaps not as often, but it's OK with me if I keep going back until the last day of my life. Why? Because there's always a gift waiting for me after I reclaim a dismembered orphan. Always.

With each visit, with each dip in the Pool of Unconditional Love, something heals, and my life expands. There are orphans left, trust me, and most of them are now old and stinky, stubborn and hateful. I handle them with all the love I can as they attempt to bully and torture me, trying to convince me to leave them alone.

Sometimes I have to get very creative and pull out my Love Blaster, a semiautomatic gun that shoots bubbles of love directly over the stubborn ones who aren't interested in accompanying me to the Pool. It totally disarms my biggest bullies. The older, tougher wounds get their turn to come home free of their suffering. THIS works!

Nineteen

My Decision to Stay

*The worst thing we can do is run away
from what what's showing up.*

- Vivian Probst

During those years that I observed my second marriage slipping away, I ached to stop it from failing. At the same time, I wasn't going to linger and suffer for the rest of my life just to keep a second "I do" promise. Once I realized that something inside *me* was part of what was happening to *us,* Life took me on the extraordinary journey to THIS.

We create what we see externally with specific purpose, even though we might not have any idea what that is. Most of what we create is happening unconsciously. So much of the time, we aren't aware of our thoughts and feelings. If we were, we would change them!

Life has provided this extraordinary tool that we call reality so that if we'll look at it, we'll know how our inner world is working, which we can then transform with conscious intervention. Therefore, **the worst thing we can do is run away from what's showing up**! Why would I leave?

Once I understood THIS, once I saw what it could do for my life, I got why leaving Tom was the worst thing I could do. I was robbing myself of the very image I needed in order to transform my inner world! What I needed desperately was to stay and observe everything that was happening in my relationship to my husband and use it to change things on Planet Me.

While I didn't know it at the time, there's a phrase for what I was doing. It's called 100 percent responsibility, and it cuts hard against ego. I had so wanted everything to be my husband's fault; I had continually blamed him for my suffering until I understood that *in every situation in life, I attracted people and circumstances that would show me what was going on inside my own self so that I could change it!*

I used to cry out, "Oh, don't show me that! It can't be inside me! That awfulness can't be mine. Go away. Better yet, I'll go. You stay." Now I say, "Thank you for showing me this."

To quote Lynne McTaggart: "the art of seeing is transforming."[74] And you can't transform what you can't see as needing to be changed.

The best thing to do—yes, THIS—when something shows up in a form I don't like I embrace it as a reflection of my inner world (and as the point of reference for this book, my husband is a powerful reflector). I love that orphan and Voila! Issues melt away. It's so amazing, and yes, it changed everything for my marriage!

Since 2008, I have been applying THIS to my life, with the most incredible results. With every visit to Planet Me, I feel more wonderful! Good things happen. I have an incredible life that I enjoy more and more without as many nasty repercussions. My marriage gets richer and more exciting. I'm so glad I didn't leave Tom; I'm so glad that Life was able to get this message to me and that I listened. There was a way to heal the wounds that so desperately needed my attention.

In truth, I don't know that I would ever have acknowledged these precious missing parts if I hadn't married Tom and stayed to learn about THIS. I'm a fan of hanging in there—in that relationship—if at all possible.

*T*o terminate a relationship before I understand my own role in its creation, growth, and development is to ask that the lesson I refuse to learn *now* be <u>postponed and magnified</u> in the future so I can better see what is being reflected back to me. I'd rather get it now than have to face it later.

To terminate a relationship because the other person reveals something that I do not want to acknowledge is to stunt my own growth, thereby requiring me to go deeper into life's lessons. Nothing disappears if I refuse to deal with it, or as Truman says in the title of her book, *Feelings Buried Alive Never Die*[75] (1991). It is always in my best interest to accept what the external world is showing me as part of my inner landscape and to nurture it and myself into a more loving space.

To blame another is the ultimate insult. In so doing, I disown what lives inside me that so desperately wants my attention. Too often I reach for blame as a weapon with which to destroy what I see, not knowing that it is my own self that suffers as a result. Following the principles of THIS, I accept that what my life partner is showing me already exists within my world.

After long years of trial and error, I stake my claim as an expert on how to have a wonderful life for myself. Because of the aid of so large a group of counselors and with such focus as the years of my life have allowed me, I have landed squarely and triumphantly (*try* with an *umph*) on my feet, profoundly settled in love.

Searching took me years; THIS happened in an instant.

The beauty of THIS is that no one has to spend years figuring it out, as long as we accept its premise—that we are all always creating our external world from our internal reality. The purpose of that outer world is to show us how we are treating ourselves in our inner world. If we want a different experience on the outside, all we have to do is change how we treat ourselves on the inside.

Any questions?

Part III

The Aftermath of THIS

Twenty

What's Science Got to Do with THIS?

Everything you think is real is not.

—Pam Grout[76]

The object and our perception of the object coincide...
our image of the world is actually a virtual creation.

—Lynne McTaggart[77]

*I*n her book *The Field*, Lynne McTaggart called quantum physics "a science of the miraculous."[78] As we dance and spin around one another, we flirt, we collide, or we send out vibrations that attract some to share in our orbit; others, we repel; and most people we won't ever make a connection with in this lifetime.

But we are all connected. McTaggart explains it this way: "Human beings and all living things are a coalescence of energy in a field of energy connected to every other living thing in the world." She referred to it as "the coming revolution" back in 2001, when her book was published. Imagine where we are today! McTaggart writes as an observer—a journalist and a detective—who has studied the concept of quantum physics and comes away from her research with an astounding announcement: "Every moment of every day we were creating our world!"

The world we see with our eyes isn't real. That's what science has known for at least sixty years, yet how easy it is for us to dismiss this as ludicrous! Wait a minute—what's ludicrous is how we resist the very truth that can change our lives into what we say we want them to be!

Niels Bohr, to whom I referred earlier, and Werner Heisenberg are legendary twentieth-century theoretical physicists and Nobel Prize winners[79]. Without them, we would not have the technological advances that we do today. Imagine life without computers, cell phones, or Internet! Our resistance to new information can hinder science from its natural forward progress; new discoveries are meant to change us—if even these revelations knock us on our butts.

We attract who and what we do because of what we think and believe about ourselves. In her book *Do You Quantum Think?* Diane Collins writes, "What you see is what you expect." Let's repeat that one more time: "What you see is what you expect." She calls it a "Voyage into Your Own Awareness."[80]. It's also a proven fact that it's what we give attention to that shows up in our world of experience!

In the first volume of his book *Conversations with God*, Neale Donald Walsch learned even more about how our world works. God apparently believes in our creative power as Walsch explains it—and it couldn't be more aligned with quantum physics. Walsch says, "The only way we can know anything about ourselves is to observe and give attention to it."[81]

Quantum science is God energy being revealed! I can't know who I am in a vacuum—none of us do, because there's nothing there to relate to. But by relating to you, I can know who I am. By seeing you—by observing any situation—*I create what I expect*. Therefore, anything I see as showing up externally to Planet Me is there so I can see what I expect—what I'm focusing on in my inner world. That's the real world.

Our physical world works tirelessly to show us this. Byron Katie says, "Everyone is a mirror of yourself—your own thinking coming back to you"[82]. I agree with her completely, but yikes! That puts me in the driver's seat for everything that's coming to pass in my life. Anyone ready for a long swim in the Pool of Unconditional Love?

I Was a Yo-Yo Wife is a peek at our most intimate relationship in which this truth is vibrantly expressed. Yes, the entire world is what we are creating to meet our expectations, but if I can improve my most intimate relationship, I believe the rest of the world will come along nicely. Dealing with just one other person is a smaller, easier context for exploring and a very powerful one.

It's exactly like that in our nonphysical world. I attract others to Planet Me to help me see who I am and to show me that I do indeed exist; **they show up as they do in order to conform to what I have expected to create!** That's why we draw others in. Hard to believe and sometimes even harder to accept.

In the words of Neale Donald Walsch, "Events, like people, are drawn to you, by you, for your own purpose."[83] I don't know about you, but my mind isn't always walking on sunshine about this. So often it would be nice to have someone else to blame, wouldn't it?

During my years of self-study, I stumbled across this concept over and over again. We are powerful, creative energy in physical form. We each contain the same powerful aspects of our Creative Source, or "The Field." So just like Life can't know Itself except through experience, we also create and attract everything that comes into our orbit in order to know ourselves and to know what lives inside of us. Only then can we resolve it with love and allow our brilliant masterpiece to be seen!

$\mathcal{S}$o what exactly did quantum physics have to do with my problems in my marriage? *Everything! It occurred to me as I studied these ideas that perhaps what I was seeing in my marriage partner was something that existed inside me—* something that I wasn't aware of—perhaps I didn't want to see. But what did that matter? My attention to it had created it; now it was showing up in my external world exactly as it was supposed to. If I could see it externally and observe it as something I wanted to change, it was up to me to do that!

Or as Lynne McTaggart further explains, "The object and our perception of the object coincide...our image of the world is actually a virtual creation."[84] I began to see it as a mirror—a reflection of what was inside me. Turns out the Law of Reflection is both a scientific and a spiritual phenomenon!

Once I grasped THIS, all blame disappeared and turned into deep gratitude. Once I was willing to acknowledge that what I saw in my beloved was a vibrational match to something inside me that needed my attention, I got busy working on the inside.

And guess what! Guess what! Things on the outside began to change. My husband turned into the most amazing man I have ever known. But I could only have that show up when I learned to "take it inside." I know he didn't have to do a thing about it—I did the work myself on the inside, but hey, if I can get a great life that way, isn't it worth it?

We can't create on the outside of our lives what doesn't exist on the inside. Let me say that inside out. What's inside always show up outside. Even if I don't want to believe it, if I will at least acknowledge it as possible, amazing changes occur. Oh, my dear husband, how could I have missed seeing how vital you are to my life?

Oh, I know; I know. If something shows up on the outside that I don't like, I want to put on my boxing gloves and pound it into the ground. I want to put on my darkest sunglasses (or my rosiest) and close my eyes so I can't see it. When everything's going well, no problem. But oh! *Don't make me face that thing that I despise!* OK. I agree. Don't face it. But do put your arms around it (even if you think it might have lice) and cradle it into the Pool of Unconditional Love, which cleans up everything—even lice can't survive!

Once we get the inside-out concept, we possess magical power. Read on if you'd like to know more about what to do once we get THIS far! I've been given tools to use that make THIS even more engaging than hiking Planet Me—secret codes (sort of) to get you to where you really want to go—to see the wonder you've felt so unworthy of.

So once again, what does science have to do with my love life? Come on; ask me this question so I can answer it. Everything! Because THIS is more than science; it's an entirely new way to see the world! We are fabulously fortunate to be alive and experiencing such a revelation. If you haven't applied this very practical science to your love life, I think you're in for a wonderful new adventure!

Twenty-One

What's God Got to Do with THIS?

Wherever you want to see the face of God, there you will see it.

—Paulo Coelho[85]

As I was learning THIS, I still had an archaic theology to overcome. Quantum physics brought me to a new understanding of "God" as an energy co-operatively working in sync with my imagination to create outcomes, rather than a mean old man pointing out all my shortcomings and punishing me for them. I was able to come out of hiding and believe in an incredible power of which I was a part and that contains all that is.

I don't know that THIS fits with *all* highly spiritual teachings; I also don't believe that's important. Yet time and again, I have come across this concept in religion and in science until I have given up all other resources as temporary and helpful but not transformative. For me, it's the alchemy of THIS that turns my experience of life into magic. For me, it's impossible to break THIS into categories or fit it into containers that we recognize. THIS for me is how Life works.

Deepak Chopra is perhaps the most highly regarded spiritual teacher on the planet. In *The Book of Secrets*[86], Chopra shares the universal principles that are the foundation of quantum physics. The "Seventh Secret" speaks so eloquently to what I have learned:

"**The events of my life reflect who I am**." Sound familiar?

"**The people in my life reflect aspects of myself**." No kidding!

"**Whatever I pay attention to will grow**." What do I want to see growing in my life?

"**Nothing is random**." Nothing.

"**At any given moment, the universe is giving me the best results possible**."

*H*ere's another quote from Abraham, the group of beings that speak to Esther Hicks.[87] It could be (probably has been) said in some other way with some other words by many spiritual leaders. Here it is verbatim:

> *I'll not ask others to become different for me...let your Vibrational Escrow percolate, and you do your best to give it your undivided attention so that you become a Vibrational Match to it. And then, when the Law of Attraction brings all of it together and brings you, because you're a match, together with it—then there aren't any bugs to work out. Don't ask the person or people that helped you to define what you want to become what you want so that you can have what you want. [Oh, that was so good.] Instead, let them be the Step One part of it (the asking part). Use your willpower and your decision to focus upon what you want—and then the Universe will bring you what you want.*

Here's my personal interpretation: "Vivian, don't ask other people to change for you—especially your husband! Focus all your attention on coming into harmony with who you are (Meology) so that the change you want to see in others will show up in the perfect way inside YOU!"

Perfect. As usual.

Twenty-Two

Practicing THIS for Life!

If it's true that what we see on the outside of our lives is an accurate reflection of our inner world, it might be time to take action to resolve the inner problem, because that's the root—the cause of the outer results. Here are some exercises I enjoy when I need to *take it inside.*

My Daily Trio

These take only a few moments each morning. I am so thrilled to share them with you!

Activity 1: The Three Gratitudes

One of my grandsons taught me this technique. Each year when it was time to open his presents for his birthday, he would get so excited that he would yell, "Thank you! Thank you! Thank you!" before opening any of them.

I loved this and decided to begin doing the same thing each morning. When my feet touch the floor each morning, I throw my arms in the air three times and declare, "Thank you! Thank you! Thank you!" It jump-starts my day. It's not important to know what gifts I'll receive that day, although I will list them later as I look back on the day.

It's so easy to think of three things I'm thankful for; in fact, I've increased the number to ten. It can be anything! I now keep a list of these in a special journal so that I can look back if I want to. Sometimes Tom will join me and create his own list as well.

Imagine what it would be like if we all did this first thing in the morning!

ACTIVITY 2: STARTING EVERY DAY IN LOVE
It's wonderful to start each day of your new vision of your life with a prayer or a quote that inspires you.

Here's mine, and I found it years ago, thanks to Neale Donald Walsch and his *Conversations with God* series[88]. It would be almost impossible not to have a wonderful life experience if you recite this to yourself every day. (By the way, this is somewhat paraphrased for my own purposes.) See what you think: "Today in each moment, my life is an extraordinary statement and an outstanding expression of the most glorious idea that I have ever had about myself. I choose the highest aspect of which I can conceive in each moment!" Isn't that just wonderful?

For a woman who saw God as a cruel taskmaster for many, many years, this was a new perspective and a healing balm. Imagine thinking God thoughts!

ACTIVITY 3: THE FABULOUS FIVE-MINUTE FOCUS
(For a copy of the Fabulous Five-Minute Focus Worksheet, visit vivianprobst. com.)

Step 1: Allow your focus to settle on an idea that you would like to see created in "reality." It could be something that you would like to see happen today or at another time. Just let it drop into your mind and write it down.

Once it is written down, put your focus on how you feel right now about your ability to make it happen, and enter that feeling-level number (see the 1–10 Feeling Scale in the Fabulous-Five Worksheet on vivianprobst.com) in the Start* column.

Example: You are a car salesperson and would like to meet a sales goal that you are having difficulty achieving. When you awaken, one of the items that might show up is meeting this goal. So the first item might read: "Meet my sales goal for the month."

Right this moment, you might think, *Yeah, right. No one is buying new cars right now. The economy sucks. It will never happen.* And then you feel quite blue about it. OK. Let's start there.

In the Start* column of your Fabulous Five-Minute Focus, you would write down a number from the Feeling Scale*— "It will never happen."

Step 2: The next step is critically simple and might feel a little strange, but do it anyway.

Focus. Close your eyes, and let your imagination take off. Allow it to play with the idea. While you feel fairly certain that it's a "no-go" right now, your thoughts and feelings would like to get out of the closet of your mind and play on the stage. Go with this. Play with the idea of possibility. Better yet, just focus, and watch your creative mind do it for you. *We dare you!*

Imagine one person coming in to the dealership today, begging you to sell them a car. Go ahead! See them insisting on paying full price and then telling you that all their friends are going to be showing up to buy cars from you, too. Ludicrous? Ridiculous? Fun? Yes!

Focus! Focus! Focus! Play it out. Let it rip! Smile, laugh, dance. See how far you can move up the Feeling Scale*, even if it is only one step. Be outrageous! (Imagine coming home at the end of the day and telling your family that you met your sales goal and the fun you had doing it.)

Step 3: Stop as soon as you start feeling better. Stop and move on to the next item. I would suggest that you allow *one minute (no more) before you move on to the next item.*

Step 4: When you've finished with all items, leave your list where you will see it at the end of the day.

And remember to take a moment to ask for a wonderful surprise. I find this particularly fun because don't we all want something to remind us that Life wants to shower us with goodness? Sometimes we are too focused on our issues, and we forget to look for the "good stuff." Putting our attention on a possible surprise can lift our spirits all day long!

<u>Step 5</u>: Each night, note anything interesting in the Progress Notes section. Prepare to be uplifted! Watch how things shift just because you took a few minutes to focus.

Many people don't have time to keep a journal. These daily lists can be retained to watch how our lives have progressed each day. It's fun!

As Needed:

Life is full of challenges. If things start leaning away from joy and wonder, I'll use any one of the following exercises to get myself back into balance.

Activity 4: Doin' the Drench

This exercise is the process I learned in Chapter 4. I am reviewing the steps here so that you can see them easily in a step-by-step format if you want to use them.

1. Imagine a place or situation in which you feel a sense of complete comfort and safety. It can be real or imaginary.

2. The important aspect of creating a place like this is that it must fully protect you and your orphans; you must feel absolutely safe here and relax in knowing that only good can come to you. Wherever or whatever it is for you, go there and soothe yourself in that feeling of complete protection. Let it drench every cell of both your being and your orphans. Often I am holding my orphan in my arms as I would a young child. In my sacred place (my Pool of Unconditional Love), I cup soothing water over it, and if it's ready for more, I either let it bathe in my pool or splash around if it wants to. Be creative—it's your very own inner world. Is it OK to say, "It's your orphan; you can do what you want to"—as long as it's full of soothing love.

3. I do this until I feel that my orphan has reintegrated into me or has healed, fully detached, and has gone home to the place it belongs.

4. If you can't imagine a place, think of a color you love and drench yourself and your orphan in that color. Wear that color if it helps!

Fragrance can help, too, so if you like a particular aroma, go for it! Oh yes, and music! Bliss!

Note: It might feel strange at first. If you've spent the early years of life being scolded, punished, and unprotected; being told you're wrong; or even being physically punished, any thought of a place of peace and protection is going to feel foreign. But you were given your imagination for a reason. You can pretend (it's a good word—*pre-tend*) whatever you want to; simply do that the best you can. With all the animated "superhero" feature films these days, one of those characters could be adopted. Captain America is my protector! Batman! Spider-Man! Mickey Mouse! (I'll need to check with my grandchildren for names of modern characters.)

In the final analysis, I believe everything about our life on earth is set up to teach us how to love ourselves. Can you believe it? It's so important to Source that it devotes almost all its energy on THIS. That's essentially what THIS is all about—it's what *life* is all about.

As we each learn to love ourselves, we enjoy life more; we offer and use our special gifts—those that we brought with us into this lifetime—and voilà! We bring more peace to our world. My work—our work—is to bring any wounded aspect of myself that is hiding out into the open and drench it in love. It might take time; I might repeat THIS over and over, but every time, there is progress—tangible, visible, and outrageous fun. Be on the lookout for miracles!

P.S. As I stated in this book, I now take time each morning to sit under the waterfall in the Pool of Unconditional Love so that my day starts with love. If there are any orphans lurking from the night before, I can reel them in before the day begins.

Activity 5: Shut Up and Color!
A sample of the Color(ing) Worksheet is available at vivianprobst.com.

Coloring has (finally) become very popular for adults and is a useful tool for quiet encounters in our inner world. I wrote *The Little Black Book for BLUE People*[89] in 2007. Back then teaching adults to color was unheard of.

The story created a very unique type of coloring, suggesting the use of just one color; the story was also compelling as it successfully taught me how to find my orphans. You can download an e-book version of this story at amazon.com. The technique I describe in the story is called Color(ing) mostly because the technique puts a person in '*ing*,' or the present moment—an important place to live from. As most of us know, the present moment is the only time we have, and it is here that everything that means anything occurs. We can color our way into the present moment with this activity.

If I come across a problem or a feeling that won't go away, and it's making me feel bad or just plain old unhappy, and I can't shake it, I start Color(ing). Here's how:

1. First, I pull out a blank sheet of paper and draw a square on it. I make the square about three inches by three inches.

2. Above the square that's three inches by three inches, I write my question or state what's bothering me. If it's about my marriage, and my husband has just humiliated me in front of another person, I might write, "What do I need to know about why my husband has humiliated me just now?" I write down whatever question comes to me.

3. I sit quietly for a moment to welcome and embrace whatever is going to show up, pondering the question a little while to give the answer time to come to me. I might even say something like, "Thank you for coming to me. I am ready to receive you and the gift you have for me."

   It can take time for gentleness to uncover something that's been living inside for perhaps a very long time. I like to think of the orphan—that sad, lonely, and neglected child. The last thing that child needs is to be chastised or told to shape up or to hurry up! It needs to be recognized and embraced. It needs soothing. Sometimes it will even speak to us! I sit quietly and listen.

4. I begin coloring the square *black*, using a colored pencil or marker. It's important not to color creatively right now. *Let all the creative energy focus on the question.* Creating designs or mixing up colors requires us

to think. *Thinking activities can destroy or distract us from the sacred process of pondering.* I simply want to use one color with a singular purpose.

5. I color slowly and thoughtfully.

6. As I color, I ask myself only one question. *What is it that I am coloring?* Then I continue coloring and allow whatever object or idea comes to my mind to do just that. I simply watch myself coloring and allow the question to answer itself. If something comes to me, I write it down.

    For example, one time I could see that my black square looked like an empty box. That's all. I wrote down, "I am coloring the inside of a black box." *Whatever you receive as an idea is a gift with a lesson or an insight.*

7. While I am in this space of allowing Life to bring me whatever treasure it has for me, I don't busy myself with other thoughts. I don't repeat any mantras or say my favorite affirmations. This is my time to listen! And color. Just keep Color(ing).

    Some people complain that they have no imagination. I refuse to accept that as true. Rather, I believe that some of us have never been permitted to use our imagination—or we have great expectations of what the imagination is. No pressure here. Whatever comes to mind is exactly what I need. Ask for your gift of knowledge, and be willing to receive it. (There are several examples of this marvelous process in *The Little Black Book for BLUE People*.)[90] If nothing comes to your mind, that's as important as anything else.

8. Once I have whatever I am given in my mind, as I keep Color(ing), I ask the next question, *What is the message of this (object)?* Or, *What does this object/idea symbolize?* Again, I just keep coloring. I continue to listen and write down what comes to me.

    For example, in the particular case that the empty box appeared to me, I wrote down, "I feel empty and depleted; no energy." It was so true that even just realizing it brought tears to my eyes and great relief!

9. When the square is fully colored, stop. (This should take no more than fifteen minutes.)

10. Now comes the best part! It's time have some fun with the colored black square. I ask, *what could I put in or add to my black square that would help me feel better?* I reach for my special colored markers that allow me to draw color on top of my black square.

Back to the example of the empty box, the question becomes, what would I love to put in or on my empty box that would make me feel good? I color that into my box. I drew some gold coins into the box and put in some colorful gemstones.

11. That's it! Color(ing) is an amazing process to bring hidden aspects of our inner world out into brilliant light! I always feel better after Color(ing)!

Consider this! *What if my spouse and I both did this exercise together? If we are feeling that our relationship is out of balance—if we're unhappy with each other— what are we really dealing with in our inner worlds?* (Perhaps a glass of wine would make this process even more enjoyable. Who can say?)

Here's what I know for sure: Whatever I'm seeing externally is trying to get me to pay (play) attention to the inside of my life. Once I get there, I can resolve whatever it is!

Activity 6: Dialing Up a Better Outcome with the "Even Better" List

I have described "The Dial" process in Chapter 5. It came to me as I was writing *Death by Roses*. In Mae Rose McElroy's afterlife, she is allowed to use "The Dial" during her Reflection (the process of looking at her most recent life). Mae Rose died and then learned to use "The Dial." However, it's a great activity to play with in this lifetime and has given me a way to find a better solution when I'm feeling stuck.

By the way, many religions believe that the time right after death includes a look-back at our lives on earth. They suggest that this is a normal part of entry into a future life. Fundamental Christianity refers to it as "The Judgment," which separates those going to heaven from those going to hell. But a number of belief systems—and certainly recent books written by those who have experienced "near death" or "death" and have come back—describe this as a way to clear our path from the old life into the new one waiting for us.

The Dial in *Death by Roses* is a literal dial that allows Mae Rose to look at the most disturbing parts of her earthly life and to "fix them" by dialing up a different (i.e., better) outcome. The Dial can move both to the right (which is more positive) or to the left (which is more negative). Mae Rose is fascinated by being able to look at earth scenes to see what options she had back then, including the options she chose during her life.

For me, the introduction of The Dial in the story was also about being able to use it during my present life, and it's been great fun. When a situation arises that looks like it's going to be a problem, I use The Dial to consider various possible paths and potential outcomes. It gives me a feeling of having choices in my response to situations rather than being forced to behave or anticipate something in a particular way. I hope you'll check it out in *Death by Roses* and perhaps use it in life. I love it so much that I think there should be a reality show about it!

Very simply, I look at the situation as it appears to be right now. Then I ask myself, *How could this improve?* I can take baby steps or giant leaps for a better way to look at what's going on.

For example, say my spouse comes home with a litany of what's gone wrong with his day. It's the last thing I want to hear (probably because I've been thinking disastrous thoughts of my own and I don't want his as well—unless I realize that he's reflecting me, and it's up to me to get myself back on track with my own wonderful life). Using The Dial, I ask myself, *How could this improve?*

Why not list a few ideas here? I'll start:

I can have compassion for my husband and for myself.
I can ask questions and help him talk out the situation.
I can practice THIS for myself to see what he might be reflecting that I need to take care of in my own life.
I can help him take his mind off the problem (never mind *how* I might do this—use your own imagination!)

I can give him time to process. (Mae Rose could have seen that Art's smoking was how he processed his problems. No, it's not a healthy habit—of course not. Instead of nagging him, she could have given him space. We all need space!)

The list goes on…right now, give some thought to how you can help "dial up" a better outcome in a situation that's challenging for you. I call it the Even Better list.

THE EVEN BETTER LIST

1) <u>State the challenge</u>: My husband repeatedly ignores my request that he put the toilet seat down.
2) <u>Now come up with one solution</u>: I could make the toilet lid spring-loaded so that when he flushes the toilet the lid automatically comes down. (It's OK to have fun with this!)
3) <u>Now try to come up with an even better idea</u>: What if I made a sticker board like we did for the kids when we were potty-training them? Come up with a reward program.
4) <u>Can I do even better?</u> Wouldn't my spouse be surprised if I stopped nagging him about it and just put the seat down myself if I notice it's up? Why is it such a big deal? Could I think of something I really appreciate about him and focus on that? (Don't be surprised if suddenly you notice that the toilet seat is being put down.)
5) <u>Oh, what about THIS?</u> What I've learned that works best for me in a situation like this (we don't have toilet seat issues in our home) is to look at that thing that my husband does that irritates the hell out of me and find something inside my inner world that this action reflects. Whatever you do, have fun with THIS!

ACTIVITY 7: CAN CHANGING YOUR NAME CHANGE YOUR LIFE?

Changing your name is not any more necessary than changing your spouse (although it *is* cheaper). I know for sure that changing my name after vowing to be true to myself has been a wonderful way to honor my transformation. Only you can decide that for yourself.

In her book of exquisite short stories, *The Stories of Eva Luna*[91], the extraordinary writer Isabel Allende describes what it meant to a fictional character in her short story "Two Words": "She went by the name Belisa Crepusculario, not because she had been baptized with that name or given it by her mother, but because she herself had searched until she found the poetry of 'beauty' and 'twilight' and cloaked herself in it."

Think about it.

When I got THIS, I decided to give up my maiden name (Theobald—I had used Theobald Probst as my last name for many years) and take only my husband's. I invited my best friends to a party to celebrate. It might sound like a non-feminist backward step, but I was weary of two last names, and I wanted to spend the rest of my life being Mrs. Probst because I treasure my marriage like never before.

Names are important. Just make sure you like yours and that it speaks well of you.

There you have it—a list of different activities I undertake to help me feel my way out of any problems or struggles that come into my life. You may already have your own, which is great. Please take time for yourself and use whatever tools are helpful so that you can truly live the wonderful life with the splendid torch you brought with you to shine in this world!

Questions

1)   What if my issue is that I can no longer stand this person?

Oh, you mean like a spouse? Thank you for asking about that! Here's what I have learned. That person is not the issue; it's what that person is showing me about my inner world that I need to accept. When I felt that my husband was treating me badly, for instance, I learned to focus on what he was reflecting to me, not on him.

Please read Byron Katie's book *Loving What Is*[92]! I love the example of the woman who couldn't bear hearing her husband breathe!

Our closest and most intimate relationship mirror what's inside of us that wants our attention—have I mentioned that? Oh yes!

So anything that shows up is a clue to your inner world! If you share this conviction, follow the process of THIS with the knowledge that the other person is not your problem; that other person is only holding a mirror for you. (Please remember what has been written about physical and sexual abuse above.) Release your messenger and go to work on your message. Could there be something inside me that I can't stand about myself? Such a tough question to ask ourselves, isn't it? But in truth, so many of us are unkind to ourselves (we sometimes call it 'being humble') that I'd look there before I do anything else.

2) *What if that person keeps showing up with the same issues over and over again?*

Yes, let's talk about that. It can be exhausting to live with something so constant in front of us! As we make progress with THIS, those events should diminish—even disappear. But during the process, we might need more of a break than locking ourselves in the bathroom or taking an overnight trip affords us. It is at these times I believe in leaving for longer periods of time—but not permanently, unless that proves to be necessary after counseling and spending time in the Pool of Unconditional Love.

It might also be true that the same issue is showing up in different people—sort of like the phrase, "Why is everybody always picking on me?" If the world is feeling that way on the outside, I'm going *inside* to see what's causing the real problem.

3) *I've already started divorce proceedings; now I feel as if I shouldn't have, especially if what you describe is true. What should I do?*

Do nothing at all, dear friend, except to go inside and find that part of yourself that needs love—that part that feels invisible, unseen, or even tormented by your partner—because in truth, it's all inside. I hope you have a wise counselor who supports and cares for you as well. The second meditation in *Three Magic Words* contains a beautiful phrase, "I simply relax in the contemplation of the good."[93]

Doesn't that sound wonderful? I see myself in a tub, leaning back and letting myself think good things. That's the secret. Just relaxing and focusing on all the good—the wonder—the possibilities. Oh, it might not stay there long—just watch how quickly it wants to jump back into the cesspool of negativity. Be gentle, and love it back with unconditional love.

If your spouse has started those proceedings against you, you can still drench yourself with love and compassion. It's just as important even if you feel like you have no control. (Perhaps it's better to say, *especially when you feel you have no control.*)

4) *THIS sounds like a lot of work. Dear Lord, if something goes wrong almost every time I am with my husband, it's ridiculous to try to put the process you've described into action!*

Not necessarily and especially because it takes hardly any time at all. If I suggest that THIS dissolved all the friction in my marriage with such immediacy that it took my breath away, you might want to give THIS a chance. It's possible that you'll see results very quickly.

Would you be willing to try THIS a few times? From the first time I tried THIS, right in the guest bedroom of our home in mid-April 2008, I noticed a major change. THIS is not to put performance pressure on anyone—it's meant to take it off by dissolving it. What I've learned is that when I really release something through THIS, it takes other appendages with it—it's better than a "two-for-one" special.

And by the way, from my experience, most work in the quantum field occurs instantaneously with little or no effort on my part except to focus and observe. I can do this while carrying on a conversation with another person because it happens in a snap!

5) *Can THIS be applied to other areas of my life in addition to my intimate relationship?*

Oh yes! My, oh my, of course! But I learned it in my marriage, and I wanted to focus on only that for this book because once I understood the idea here, I could, and do, apply it in other ways. Just don't get carried away with concern. Life wants us to have fun, and getting bogged down thinking about THIS is exactly the opposite. Use it only when issues show up. It's quick and effective.

6) *You're suggesting that over time, the smaller issues "dissolve" and the older, more stubborn ones remain. Is that what I should expect in my experience if I begin to work with* THIS?

I can't honestly say what THIS will do for you or how you will experience it. We are all unique, and that makes the process different for everyone.

For me, anxiety is probably one of the oldest and most major orphans I have. Last night my husband was driving us to our hotel in Montevideo, Argentina. It was dark; there were a lot of cars darting around and people dressed in dark clothes crossing streets. It was a perfect setup for an anxiety attack for me.

As I did my breathing exercises, I also focused on THIS. I asked simply that all the anxieties of my life come forward and attach to this event so that all could be drenched together. We finally arrived safely at our hotel, and I was very relieved. Many of us have major life issues, and we have no idea where they came from. I use THIS to soothe myself and notice major shifts when I do.

Another example is that we are traveling in South America, and our knowledge of Spanish is very limited. Ever since learning a foreign language when I was a foreign-exchange student, I have never wanted to use it to try to communicate because I have always felt so inferior and stupid. But on this trip? The first one we've taken since I studied THIS? Oh la la! I am so enjoying trying to communicate in a different language. Everyone smiles and appreciates my efforts.

Oh, and dancing…since working with THIS, I am no longer so shy about being seen dancing. Can you believe all the years that (a) I was told that dancing was sinful, and (b) when I decided I wanted to try it, I was so terrified of what I would look like to others?

OK. So Tom and I didn't try the tango in Buenos Aires (Tom said it would put him in traction), but we attended an incredible show full of tango dancing, and I danced my ass off (admittedly without tangoing) at a wedding among friends in Puerto Vallarta. What a blast!

THIS has blown the lid off so many things I have avoided during my lifetime; the sense of freedom is incredible. Who knows where THIS can or will take me or you? Does it make you want to find out?

7. *OK, Vivian, thanks for sharing, but you've left a large portion of the population out of this book. I'm single. I don't have an intimate partner. Are you telling me that I therefore can't benefit from THIS?*

Not at all. I have written this as a memoir, and my experience of THIS occurred in my marriage, but THIS probably works in all different kinds of scenarios. Those who are not married (and who are sometimes greatly envied by those who are—just so you know) may not have to look very far to find provocative experiences that can put THIS to work. The fact that someone isn't sharing a bed with me doesn't make THIS irrelevant.

Married, single, or any other state, THIS is fundamentally about seeing both what delights and what bothers us as we observe life around us, and understanding that the same terrain lives inside of us. It's also about remembering that even if we see it on the outside, the fix is most likely on the inside first.

Close friends, people at work, children, relatives, customers, clients—by simply observing who and what is showing up in our lives we can benefit from THIS.

By the way, did it ever occur to you that perhaps you don't need the "in-your-face reflection" that those of us who are married do? Maybe that's why being single is the best life for you right now? You can study your Meology to your heart's content! But if you're lonely and wishing you had a partner, perhaps there's a lonely orphan inside that needs attention and, once drenched with love, might dissolve any obstacles that stand in the way.

Epilogue

om and I have a wonderful life and relationship, but we do not live in Nirvana, nor have we reached a blissful state where nothing ever goes wrong. In fact, Tom and I do not agree on some very fundamental levels. I can't even say that he agrees with me about THIS, and he doesn't have to.

Tom rises early, goes to work, and looks at the problems he faces as reality—not personal but often burdensome. He seeks the best practical solution based on what he trusts and believes. He doesn't take things personally in the way I do. They are external, as are the reasons for the circumstances that he faces.

I begin the day later than he does; I sit in gratitude and quiet before I go into the office. I see everything external as deeply personal. Whatever happens in my life comes from a place within, and I ask for its lesson. I see that I am creating much wonder and beauty, and I'm experiencing inexplicable joy more often than not.

But I do not live in conflict with Tom, even though we often disagree about how to approach something. I don't believe that partners in a relationship have to agree, compromise, give in, or change in order to live in a happy, satisfying marriage. It is so much fun to explore our differences. I have learned so much from Tom, and perhaps he from me as well. I even agree with him sometimes. Perhaps it is most important to say that while I believe everyone would benefit from seeing the world from THIS perspective, which I have come to cherish because it gives me the greatest power from which to live my life, I am only responsible for myself in this regard.

There is great strength in a relationship that allows for differences—that not only accepts them but embraces them. Tom enables me to see myself so clearly, and I treasure that. It doesn't matter that we have different opinions— what matters is how I can see my personal inner life through our relationship and thereby enhance my clarity about my life. It also matters that there is so much that is good between us that it is becoming rarer for us to have conflicts, and they surprise both of us when they come up.

Just the other day we were traveling together, and I saw another car coming into our lane, which caused me alarm. I cried out to Tom in my fear, and he responded by rather curtly informing me that he knew what was going on and that he had everything under control. I felt rebuked by him and was instantly angry that he didn't respond to me with any sense of love or even gratitude that I had brought this to his attention. Tom is an excellent driver, but I was concerned that he didn't know what was happening. And I was afraid there would be an accident.

His response triggered immediate great rage inside me, which I expressed. Then I fell silent, for I knew that what was going on inside me needed my attention. Why would I feel afraid? Why would I feel belittled by him when I expressed my fear?

It didn't take long for me to find the source of my reaction. From a very, very young age, I had known great fear: fear of my mother's rage; fear that my parents didn't understand how very lonely and afraid I was; and fear of punishment, both temporal and eternal. I was so often rebuked for something that caused my mother to be angry even if I wasn't doing anything wrong. To be punished in this way can leave lifelong scars unless we learn how to heal ourselves.

Tom's response in that moment brought all of this forward. As we drove quietly awhile, I went through THIS process and recognized—aha! —another area that Life wanted me to see clearly so that I could soothe it with love, which I did.

As I soothed myself and loved that part of me that was so devastated by being misunderstood, I came into a more incredible connection with myself. I saw the frightened, innocent little child; I saw the anger incited in me because I felt Tom didn't understand. Then I also saw that all this was for me to bring that fearful, neglected aspect of myself into my heart and soul with great love and compassion.

I have never felt that others understood the fear that has lived inside me for most of my life. But what came out of this singular incident was that *I also despised myself for feeling this way.* So my lesson was to seize the opportunity to drench that insecurity with love, which I did. Another long-standing problem was being healed by THIS process!

Life wants us to love and accept ourselves in all aspects. I believe Life wants us to take the events of our lives very personally—to know that power we have to create and to use these events for our highest good. It is those places that we don't want to visit inside us—those orphans we have cut ourselves away from—that we need to welcome back. Life will be faithful to bring us back to ourselves.

I bless each of these opportunities to grow deeper into my life and to grow stronger in loving myself and appreciating who I am underneath the layers of protection I have hidden under for so many years. One of our greatest teachers is contrasting experience, which gives us a framework within which to define ourselves. *Conflict is simply resistance to all the wonder we have yet to experience.* Whether it's a world at war with itself or a person at war with himself or herself, the way to peace and ultimate freedom for me has been through understanding THIS one thing that changes everything.

In *I Was a Yo-Yo Wife*, I have attempted to share what I learned that changed my relationship first with myself and then with my husband. It also felt important to give readers the backdrop of my life in order to orient them. If I had had a different life, I would have had a different story to tell.

In fact, my focus has been informed by my life experience. It would have been nearly impossible for me to learn THIS one thing that changed everything if I had had an easy childhood and a glorious first marriage. But I believe that's exactly the point. We are each given lives to live on purpose. Without the unique and precise lessons, we learn as we live, we would not be able to shine our lights nearly so well. Had I not suffered abuse, I would not be compassionate; had I not left a way of life that did not serve the woman I was to become, I would have lived a dishonest life; if I hadn't put myself out into the world to tell my story, no one could have benefited from what I have learned.

I hope this book has been helpful. I hope those of you who have taken on the challenge of studying your life through Meology (or whatever form works for you) have a deeper, richer sense of yourselves and the gifts you bring.

For those of you who suffer the pain of a relationship that does not support you, I hope that working with THIS brings you the hoped-for transformation you so desire. But most of all, I hope you never stop in one place and say that there is nothing left to learn, nothing more to offer or that nothing works.

Be very, very good to this human being that you are; give it time off to bask in the essence of all Life wants to give you. Let yourself enjoy being who you are, and embrace a world in which all of us are learning to do just that!

Don't hide, don't wilt, and whatever you do, remember THIS!

End Notes

1. "Life" is the term I use throughout this book to signify the inner guidance that is available to all of us—that source of our existence that lives and breathes through us.

2. No one agrees on the actual statistics. The sites I referred to are The U.S. Census Bureau and the National Center for Disease Control. I noted that a number of websites use this data. Glenn Stanton, "Sharing Divorce Statistics" http://winst.org, (December 6, 2015).
See also http://www.FastStats-Marriage and Divorce-CDC (June 13, 2016).
See also http://www.cdc.gov. This site indicates that between 2000-2015, the number of marriages per 1,000 people decreased from 8.2 to 6.9, a decrease of 1.3 per 1,000. Divorces decreased during the same timeframe from 4.0 per 1,000 to 3.1 per thousand, a decrease of .9 per 1,000. While this raw data does not translate exactly, it demonstrates that the decline in the number of marriages exceeds the decline in the number of divorces.

3. Ibid.

4. "32 Shocking Divorce Statistics" http://mckinleyirvin.com (October 30, 2012) "Being previously married markedly elevates one's risk of divorce."

5. Merriam Webster Dictionary: Dictionary and Thesaurus. January 30, 2017; On-line @ www.merriam-webster.com.

6. "*Marriage* and related terms are used to indicate all committed relationships regardless of their legal definition."

7. "AOL Poll Reveals Majority of Married Women Would Reconsider Their Spouses: 36% Would not Marry Their Husbands If They Could Re-DO Their I DO' and Another 20% Not Sure. http://www.prnewswire.com/news-releases/womans-dayaol-poll-reveals-majority-of-married-women-would-reconsider-their-spouses-36-would-not-marry-their-husbands-if-they-could-re-do-their-i-do--another-20-not-sure-53289747.html (January 2, 2007).

8. Digh, Patti. *Creative is a Verb.* (Guilford:Globe Pequot Press, 2011), 175-179.

9. Fitzpatrick, Richard. July 14, 2007. "Law of Reflection." http://www.physicsclassroom.com/class/refln/Lesson-1/The-Law-of-Reflection.

10. Names changed to protect privacy.

11. Founded in 1977, the Women's Center of Waukesha, WI has claimed status as one of the leading centers for women in transition. For information visit twc.org.

12. McTaggart, Lynne, *The Field,* New York: Harper. 2001.

13. Define quantum mechanics: physics: a branch of physics that deals with the structure and behavior of very small pieces of matter. https://www.merriam-webster.com/dictionary/quantum%20mechanics

14. "Webmaster is not alone in failing to find a primary source. Regardless of how widely quoted, the few citations to be found merely reference other books in which it is stated without a valid citation. For example, this quote is an epigraph in Eric Middleton, *The New Flatlanders* (2007), 19, with a note (p.151) citing Niels Bohr, *Atomic Physics and Human Knowledge* (1958), but Webmaster's search of that text does not find it." See also Heisenberg, Werner, 1972. *Physics and Beyond: Encounters and Conversations,* (World Perspective Series, Volume #42)

15. Katie, Byron, *Loving What Is,* New York: Harmony Books. 2002

16. Deepak Chopra has explained the Vibrational Permission Zone this way, "The universe is forced to accept your boundaries." Chopra, Dr. Deepak, *The Book of Secrets: Unlocking the Hidden Dimensions of Your Life.* New York; Three Rivers Press, 2004), p. 234.

17. There are many books focused on the study of quantum physics. Some of the easiest authors to follow are Fred Allen Wolf, Pam Grout, and Greg Kuhn.

18. Richo, Dr. David, *When The Past Is Present: Healing the Emotional Wounds that Sabotage Our Relationships.* Boston & London; SHAMBHALA, 2008), p. 1.

19. Ibid. #18

20. https://www.amazon.com/Inner-Peace-Cards-Wayne-Dyer/dp/1561707864

21. Hicks, Jerry and Esther, Untitled. The quotation was excerpted from San Diego, California, on July 31, 1999, and appeared on the Abraham-Hicks "Daily Law of Attraction" subscription site. http://www.abraham-hicks.com/lawofattractionsource/dqsubscribe.php Abraham is a group of spirit guides from the 'other side' who speak through Esther Hicks.

22. King, Stephen, *On Writing: A Memoir of the Craft;* New York; Scribner; 2000. P. 37, 163

23. For more information, visit www.whenwordscount.com

24. Lerner, Harriet, *Dance of Anger.* New York: Harper & Row, 1985. This word split is original with me. In fact, I'm not sure that any of my word-splits are, but they show up in my head from time to time and certainly make English interesting!

25. Maulana Jalaluddin Rumi was a 13th century Persian poet, an Islamic dervish and a Sufi mystic. He is regarded as one of the greatest spiritual masters and poetical intellects. Born in 1207 AD, he belonged to a family of learned theologians. See Rumi Biography - Childhood, Life Achievements & Timeline. http://*www.thefamouspeople.com/profiles/rumi-20.php*

26. Ibid. #18

27. "Electroconvulsive therapy (ECT) is a procedure, done under general anesthesia, in which small electric currents are passed through the brain, intentionally triggering a brief seizure. ECT seems to cause changes in brain chemistry that can quickly reverse symptoms of certain mental illnesses." See http:www.mayoclinic.org/tests-procedures/electroconvulsive-therapy/basics/definition/prc-20014161 While the treatment did not appear to work for my mother, others have benefited.

28. #19, Ibid.

29. Hamilton, David C. d.hamilton.jungiananalyst@gmail.com "Jungian Analysis is the psychotherapeutic approach of Analytical Psychology in which the analyst and patient work together to bring unconscious elements of the psyche into a more balanced relationship with conscious awareness and experience in an effort to discover meaning, facilitate maturation of the personality, ..."http://www.jungiananalystvt.com/HowdoesJungianAnalysisWork.en.html, (2016)

30. Thompson, Joyce A. MS, LMFT, *"Childhood Trauma and the Mind-Body Connection for Adults"* http:// www.goodtherapy.org/blog/psychotherapy-childhood-trauma-mind-body/ (Feb 16, 2010)

31. Please refer back to Chapter 4 for details on the process I was taught.

32. Eye Movement Desensitization and Reprocessing (EMDR) is a psychotherapy treatment that was originally designed to alleviate the distress associated with traumatic memories. https://www.emdr.com/what-is-emdr/

33. Lyricists, Jim Cocoran and Benoit Justras, (Josh Groban, 2001).

34. Ibid. # 25

35. Wolf, Fred Alan, PhD. "Awakening your Soul or: Becoming aware that you are a Spiritual Universe", http://fredalanwolf.com/myarticles/awakening

36. Truman, Karol K., *Feelings Buried Alive Never Die,* Saint George: Olympus Distributing. (1991).

37. Wondra, Anne, *Relationship Rules of a Happy Woman,* Waukesha. 2016.

38. Shaw, George Bernard, Irish comic dramatist, literary critic, and socialist propagandist, winner of the Nobel Prize for Literature in 1925.More at *https://www.britannica.com/biography/George-Bernard-Shaw*

39. Myss, Caroline, *Sacred Contracts: Awakening Your Diving Potential,* New York: Harmony Books. 2001.

40. Ibid., #35

41. Cameron, Julia, *The Vein of Gold: A Journey to Your Creative Heart* New York: Jeremy P. Tarcher/Putnam. 1996.

42. Bolles, Richard, *What Color is Your Parachute* California: Ten Speed Press. 1970

43. Ibid. #41.

44. Buscaglia, Leo, *Living, Loving & Learning,* New Jersey: Charles B. Slack Inc. 1982.

45. http://www.myersbriggs.org. There are many types of personality tests on the market. This is probably the oldest and most credible (my opinion). My life changed when I got the results of my test; what a relief it was to have a better sense of who I was and to give myself permission to live from that place.

46. Ibid. #42.

47. Gawain, Shakti, *Creative Visualization,* Mill Valley: Whatever Publishing. 1986.

48. Wheatly, Margaret J. *Leadership and the New Science: Learning about Organization from an Orderly Universe.* San Francisco: Berrett-Koehler Publishers. 1992.

49. Wheatley, Margaret J. and Kellner-Rogers, Myron, *A Simpler Way,* San Francisco: Berrett-Koehler Publishers. 1996.

50. Ibid, #33.

51. Christiansen, Beth, *Daily Meditations: 100 Days of Love and Light for Your Spiritual Growth,* (Milwaukee: Radiant Heart Press. 2014.

52. Ibid. #16.

53. Cameron, Julia, *The Artist's Way,* New York: G.P. Putnam's Sons. 1992.

54. A short biography of Dr. Matthews appears at the end of this book.

55. Blake, William, *The Marriage of Heaven and Hell,* (Engraved by Blake's wife in 1790; London & New York: Oxford University Press. 1908.

56. Jung, Carl, *The Self,* (Aion. Volume 9, Part II of *The Collected Works of C. G. Jung.*) Princeton: Princeton University Press. (1948)1978.

57. The term "People of the Book" in the Koran refers to followers of mono-theistic Abrahamic religions that are older than Islam. This includes all Christians, all Children of Israel (including Jews, Karaites, and Samaritans), and Sabians (definition from Wikipedia).

58. Ibid. #51. *"A Review of Complex Theory".* (Volume 8 of *The Collected Works of C.G. Jung. Edited by Sir Herbert Read, Michael Fordham, Gerhard Adler, and William McGuire.*) Princeton: Princeton University Press. (1934)1978. See also *Letters to William Kinney;* Princeton: Princeton University Press. 1975 (May 27, 1956).

59. Go to the Religious Tolerance website, http://www.religioustolerance.org/reciproc2.html for many versions of this rule.

60. Erickson, Erik H., *Adulthood,* New York: W. W. Norton. Ed 1978.

61. Ibid. #58.

62. Runaway Bride, 1999 directed by Garry Marshall, and stars Julia Roberts and Richard Gere. The screenplay was written by Josann McGibbon and Sara Parriott

63. Ibid. #16.

64. Anderson, U.S. *Three Magic Words,* Hollywood: Wilshire Book Company. 1954.

65. Ibid. #15.

66. Ibid. #15.

67. Simon, Paul, *Negotiations and Love Songs*. 1971-86. Compact disc. Produced by Muscle Shoals Sound Rhythm Section, tracks A4-B1

68. Cameron, Julie, *The Artist's Way*, New York: G.P. Putnam's Sons. 1992.

69. Northrup, Dr. Christiane, *The Wisdom of Menopause*, New York: Bantam Books. 2001.

70. Kumar, Dr. Kalpana (Rose), *Becoming Real: Harnessing the Power of Menopause for Health and Success*. Pewaukee: Medial Press.

71. This short-story book by Vivian Probst is available on Amazon.

72. Green Card, a 1991 romantic film written, produced, directed by Peter Weir and starring Gérard Depardieu and Andie MacDowell.

73. As of January 28, 2017, Mort Fertel's website is easily accessible by typing Mort Fertel into your search engine. His website is www.marriagemax. com.

74. Ibid. #12.

75. Ibid. #35.

76. Grout, Pam, *E2*, New York: Hay House. 2013.

77. Ibid. #12

78. Ibid. #12.

79. Ibid. #13.

80. Collins, Diane, *Do You Quantum Think?* New York: Select Books. 2011.

81. Walsch, Neale Donald, *Conversations with God, Book 1.* New York: G.P. Putnam's Sons.

82. Ibid. #15.

83. Ibid. #61.

84. Ibid. #12.

85. Coelho, Paulo. Quoted from one of the many books of his I have read. Could not locate exact citation.

86. Ibid. #16.

87. Ibid. #19.

88. Ibid. #75.

89. Probst, Vivian, *The Little Black Book for BLUE People,* Pewaukee: LifeMark Press. 2007.

90. Ibid. #83.

91. Allende, Isabel, *The Stories of Eva Luna,* New York: Atria Books. 1987.

92. Ibid. #15.

93. Ibid. #60.

Bibliography

Allende, Isabel. 1987. *The Stories of Eva Luna.* New York: Atria Books.

Andersen, U. S. 1954. *Three Magic Words.* Hollywood: Wilshire Book Company.

AOL Online. January 2, 2007. "AOL Poll Reveals Majority of Married Women Would Reconsider Their Spouses: 36% Would Not Marry Their Husbands If They Could Re-Do Their 'I DO' & Another 20% Not Sure." AOL OnlineS. January 25, 2017, prnewsire.com/news-releases/ Womans-dayaol-poll.

Bolles, Richard. 1970. *What Color is Your Parachute?* California: Ten Speed Press.

Cameron, Julia. 1996. *The Vein of Gold: A Journey to Your Creative Heart.* New York: Jeremy P. Tarcher/Putnam.

Cameron, Julia. 1992. *The Artist's Way.* New York: G. P. Putnam's Sons.

Chopra, Deepak. 2004. *The Book of Secrets.* New York: Harmony Books.

Collins, Diane. 2011. *Do You Quantum Think?* New York: SelectBooks Inc.

Digh, Patti. 2011. *Creative Is a Verb.* Guilford: Globe Pequot Press.

Dyer, Wayne W. 2004. *Staying on the Path.* Carlsbad, CA: Hay House.

Erikson, Erik H., ed. 1978. *Adulthood.* New York: W. W. Norton.

Fitzpatrick, Richard. July 14, 2007. "Law of Reflection." http://www.phys-icsclassroom.com/class/refln/Lesson-1/The-Law-of-ReflectionGawain, Shakti. 1986. *Creative Visualization.* Mill Valley: Whatever Publishing.

Grout, Pam. 2013. *E2.* New York: Hay House.

(Heisenberg, 1971). *Physics and Beyond.* World Perspectives.

Hicks, Jerry and Esther, July 31, 1999, Untitled, . Abraham – Hicks Publications/ Online subscription service.

www.abraham-hicks.com/lawofattractionsource/dqsubscribe.php

Jung, C. G. (1948) 1978. "The Self." *Aion.* Vol. 9, Part II of *The Collected Works of C. G. Jung.* Princeton: Princeton University Press.

(1934) 1978. "A Review of the Complex Theory." Vol. 8 of *The Collected Works of C. G. Jung.* Edited by Sir Herbert Read, Michael Fordham, Gerhard Adler, and William McGuire. Princeton: Princeton University Press. 1975. 26 May 1956. In *Letters to William Kinney.* Princeton: Princeton University Press.

Katie, Byron. 2002. *Loving What Is.* New York: Harmony Books.

King, Stephen. 2000. *On Writing: A Memoir of the Craft.* New York: Scribner.

Kellner-Rogers, Myron. 1996. *A Simpler Way.* San Francisco: Berrett-Koehler Publishers.

Kumar, Kalpana (Rose). 2011. *Becoming Real: Harnessing the Power of Menopause for Health and Success.* Pewaukee: Medial Press.

McTaggart, Lynne. 2001. *The Field.* New York: Harper.

Northrup, Christiane. 2001. *The Wisdom of Menopause.* New York: Bantam Books.

Probst, Vivian. 2007. *The Little Black Book for BLUE People.* Pewaukee: LifeMark Press.
2008. *The TimeMaker's Shop.* Pewaukee: LifeMark Press.
2015. *Death by Roses.* New York: Select Books.

Richo, David. 2008. *When the Past Is Present.* Boston and London: SHAMBHALA.

Shaw, George Bernard. n.d. "A Splendid Torch."

Simon, Paul. *Negotiations and Love Songs.* 1971–86, compact disc.

Thompson, Julia. 2010. "Childhood Trauma and the Mind-Body Connection for Adults." GoodTherapy.org. Accessed January 25, 2017. http://www. goodtherapy.org/blog/psychotherapy-childhood-trauma-mind-body/

Truman, Karol K. 1991. *Feelings Buried Alive Never Die.* Saint George: Olympus Distributing.

Walsch, Neale Donald. 1995. *Conversations with God, Book 1.* New York: G. P. Putnam's Sons.

Wheatley, Margaret J. 1992. *Leadership and the New Science: Learning about Organization from an Orderly Universe.* San Francisco: Berrett-Koehler Publishers.

Wondra, Anne. 2016. *Relationship Rules of a Happy Woman.* Waukesha: Anne Wondra.

About the Authors

Vivian Probst

Vivian Probst is an award-winning author and speaker whose message comes from an inner fire that compels her to search out the unique brilliance of every human being. She "suited up" for this work with a deeply religious background and early training in culture and linguistics.

A former missionary, then a displaced homemaker living in poverty, Probst rose to become a national consultant to the affordable-housing industry. She has captured the hearts of thousands with her unique gift of insight, humor, and passion to bring out the best of who we *really* are through her seminars and stories.

Since 2013, Probst has been a certified practitioner of Akashic records. She lives in Wisconsin.

Boris Matthews

Boris Matthews practices as a Jungian psychoanalyst in Madison and Milwaukee, Wisconsin. He regularly teaches in the Analyst Training Program at the C. G. Jung Institute of Chicago, where he also supervises analysts-in-training and works on various committees. Matthews earned a PhD in German, earned a master's degree in social work, and completed his analytic training in Chicago in 1987.

61225161R00137

Made in the USA
Lexington, KY
04 March 2017